Storytelling
Branding in Practice

Klaus Fog · Christian Budtz
Baris Yakaboylu

Storytelling

Branding
in Practice

 Springer

Klaus Fog
Christian Budtz
Baris Yakaboylu

SIGMA
Wilders Plads 15C
1403 Copenhagen
Denmark
sigma@sigma.dk

*Original Danish edition published
by Samfundslitteratur 2003 with the
title Storytelling-branding i praksis
(Klaus Fog, Christian Budtz, Baris
Yakaboylu), 1. udgave 2002, 2. oplag
2003. Translation by Tara Stevens.*

Cataloging-in-Publication Data applied for
Library of Congress Control Number: 2004114981
 A catalog record for this book is available from the Library of Congress.

Bibliographic information published by Die Deutsche Bibliothek
Die Deutsche Bibliothek lists this publication in the Deutsche Nationalbibliografie;
detailed bibliographic data available in the internet at *http://dnb.ddb.de*

ISBN 3-540-23501-9 Springer Berlin Heidelberg New York

Springer is a part of Springer Science+Business Media
springeronline.com

© Springer-Verlag Berlin Heidelberg 2005
Printed in Denmark

Cover design: Erich Kirchner, Heidelberg
Production: Helmut Petri
Printing: Narayana Press

SPIN 11605928   Printed on acid-free paper – 42/3153 – 5 4 3 2

Contents

PART TWO: STORYTELLING APPLIED

Chapter 6: Storytelling as a Management Tool 124

Chapter 7: Storytelling in Advertising 150

Foreword

Today's world is overflowing with fancy buzzwords. The vast majority of them however, refer to short-lived phenomena that have been invented for the sole purpose of selling hot air. They are gone as quickly as they arrived. Others, are a product of the times, but have deeper roots. They touch upon something familiar, but contribute to a new consciousness, and take a firm hold in our future vocabulary. "Storytelling" is one of them.

At the European based communication unit SIGMA, we have been helping companies to build their brands by finding their unique story since 1996. At that time, it was called PR, communication, advertising or marketing. Today the lines dividing those categories have blurred. But at the very core of all that we do, is our deep belief in the inherent power of telling a company's unique story. Along the way, we have found that companies are increasingly interested in this subject, but, that there is also confusion as to what the term actually means when it comes to its practical application. For this reason, we have written a book, which shares our experiences of branding through storytelling, offering practical tools that provide a good starting point for companies to tell stories of their own.

The book came to life in a bustling loft in Copenhagen, Denmark, during the heat wave of the summer of 2002. It is the result of years of experience, new ideas, ups and downs, late nights and early mornings, praise and criticism. Many people have been involved in its conception. First and foremost our thanks to Kjeld Kirk Kristiansen, CEO, the LEGO Company, Lars Kolind, former CEO of Oticon, and Torben Ballegaard Sørensen, CEO of Bang and Olufsen for their courage in taking our advice to heart; that a good story is the key to global success.

Their faith, meant that we at SIGMA received confirmation of the powerful effect a story has when told in the right way, to the right people at the right time.

We must also thank Morten Jonas, Hanne Andersen, Klavs Hjort and Claus Moseholm, who during their time with SIGMA, contributed thoughts and ideas that form the basis of this book. Also a heartfelt thank you to Tara Stevens and Kurt Pitzer who on many occasions have travelled to Denmark from London, L.A., Bosnia and Barcelona to help us in our search for the good story. Thank you to all the people at SIGMA who have contributed with input and support. A special thank you to Tue Paarup for his keen model development and his critical and clarifying feedback. To Trine Mollgaard for constructive criticism, Peter Thielst Jessen for inspired graphic design, Thomas Thorhauge for his amazing illustrations, to Julie Thygesen for research, and to Tara Stevens and Niels Blom for translating the book into English.

For comments and feedback we must also thank Eva Lykkegaard, Christian Schou, Glen Jacobsen and Christine Antorini. Thanks to Ken Harper for inspirational dialogue on digital storytelling and Henrik Schjerning from Samfundslitteratur. And to futurologist Rolf Jensen for his pioneering work in bringing storytelling to the attention of the business community, while we were busy implementing it in practice.

Finally we owe a debt of heartfelt gratitude to Julie, Lykke, Iluuna, Markus, Anna, David, Sarah and Tine for their patience, love and support.

This is our contribution to everybody who makes it his or her daily task to chase the good story.

Happy hunting!

September 2004 – SIGMA, Copenhagen, Denmark

Branding Through Storytelling 1

"It was an unusually busy afternoon at the local Domino's Pizza in small town America. Orders were coming in at a blistering pace, the kitchen was at maximum capacity and the blue-uniformed delivery boys and girls were working overtime to get pizzas out to hungry customers. It was just then that the unthinkable happened: they were nearly out of pizza dough. Stocks were so low in fact, that if orders kept coming in at the frenzied pace they had been doing so, the kitchen would simply run out. Action was needed, and fast.

The manager grabbed the phone and called the national Vice President of Distribution for the US, explaining the situation. A chill ran down the spine of the Vice President as he thought of the public embarrassment if one of Domino's outlets could not deliver as promised. Springing into action, he did everything in his power to solve the problem: A private jet was dispatched at once, laden with Domino's special deep pan dough, and all the while local employees battled against the clock, as their inventory of dough dwindled.

Unfortunately, all their efforts were in vain. Even a private jet couldn't get the dough there on time, and that night Domino's Pizza was forced to disappoint many hungry customers. For an entire month afterwards, employees went to work wearing black mourning bands."

It is not a particularly happy ending, but we are left in no doubt as to the importance Domino's Pizza place on their ability to deliver. After all, it is their commitment to this promise that the brand is built on. And the message within this particular story resonates strongly throughout the organisation giving employees a very clear idea of what their brand values are, while showing consumers exactly what promise lies at the heart of the Domino's brand.

Herein, lays the true power of a good story. Even this relatively small anecdote has depth, credibility and a punchy message applicable to both internal and external listeners. It makes it easier for us to believe in Domino's vision: to be "the best pizza delivery company in the world". By telling a story like this, both employees and consumers understand what it really means to be the best.

As a concept, storytelling has won a decisive foothold in the debate on how brands of the future will be shaped. Yet, there is still a conspicuous lack of critical insight as to how and why storytelling can make a difference. For most companies, storytelling remains an abstract concept, at best reserved for PR and advertising executives, at worst, wishy-washy claptrap with no real value: What's the point of telling stories anyway? What makes a good story? And how do you go about telling it so that it supports the company brand?

As a concept, storytelling has won a decisive foothold in the debate on how brands of the future will be shaped.

Concrete answers are few and far between, and the debate for now is largely academic. The aim of this book is to make storytelling tangible. In the following chapters, we hope to turn abstract notions of storytelling into practical tools by giving real-life examples of how storytelling can be used as an effective branding tool.

This book is written for those of you who are fed up with lofty talk, and for those of you who are interested in using storytelling as a branding tool within your company.

Once Upon a Time...

In days of old when we were still hunters and gatherers, and our social lives took place around the glow of a campfire, women prepared the evening meal while their men folk swapped stories of the day's hunt. It was here too, that the tribe's elders handed down the myths and legends surrounding their gods and ancestors and where knowledge and experience was exchanged and passed along the generations. These stories helped shape the identity of the tribe, gave it values and boundaries and helped establish its reputation among rivalling tribes. It was storytelling in its purest form.

In many ways the modern company resembles these tribes of old: the stories that circulate in and around the organisation paint a picture of the company's culture and values, heroes and enemies, good points and bad, both towards employees and customers. By sharing our stories, we define "who we are" and "what we stand for". And just like the elders of the tribes of old, the strong leaders of today's companies distinguish themselves by being good storytellers; voices that employees listen to, are inspired by and respect.

Indeed, storytelling is an integral part of what distinguishes us as human beings. The esteemed writer and movie director, Paul Auster, once said that telling stories is the only way we can create meaning in our lives and make sense of the world. We need them in order to understand ourselves and communicate who we are. And by sharing stories of our experiences, we can better understand the conflicts of our daily lives and find explanations for how we fit into this world.

Since time began, religious stories have provided people with deeper meaning in life.

Since time began, religious stories have provided people with deeper meaning in life, offering insight into why we are here and how we should live, and providing comfort in our darker times. The Bible is perhaps the most obvious example of this.

but in order for this conflict to play out, you need a cast of interacting and compelling characters.

The classical fairy-tale is built on a fixed structure where each character has a specific role to play in the story, and each person supplements each other and forms an active part of the story. This classical structure can be found in storytelling traditions throughout the Western world – from old-fashioned folk tales to Hollywood's action packed blockbusters. The structure of the classical fairy-tale (figure 2.3) highlights each individual character, and their functions and roles in relation to each other.

A classical structure can be found in storytelling traditions throughout the Western world – from old-fashioned folk tales to Hollywood's action packed blockbusters.

A story typically starts out with your main character or *hero* pursuing a *goal*. Let us say, the hero is Robin Hood fighting for justice and freedom in England. The hero has one or more arms of *support*, in this case, Little John and his merry men. But he also has certain special skills; an acute sense of cunning, and a bow and arrow, which also support his quest.

The hero's path to achieving his goal, however is not problem-free. There is always an *adversary* who tries to work against the hero, thereby establishing the conflict. In the case of Robin Hood, his adversaries are Prince John and the Sheriff of Nottingham who must be defeated in order for justice to prevail. A deeper interpretation is that Prince John is a personification of cruelty and the abuse of power in England. *The benefactor* is King Richard, who, in the end returns from the crusades establishing peace and justice in England. And *the beneficiary* in this story is England, in particular the poor and oppressed who have suffered under the yoke of Prince John's rule. In short: A classic cast of characters that give the story its structure. When developing your own corporate stories, you can benefit from using the Fairy-tale Model to check if your story has the necessary characters to pull the story together.

When developing your own corporate stories, you can benefit from using the Fairy-tale Model to check if your story has the necessary characters to pull the story together.

Generally speaking a successful conflict needs a hero and a villain with opposing agendas. The adversary can take on many guises, both physical and psychological. It could for example be a static obstacle such as a mountain that must be scaled, but on a deeper level shows the real adversary to be the fear of climbing that mountain.

Figure 2.3

The Fairy-tale Model

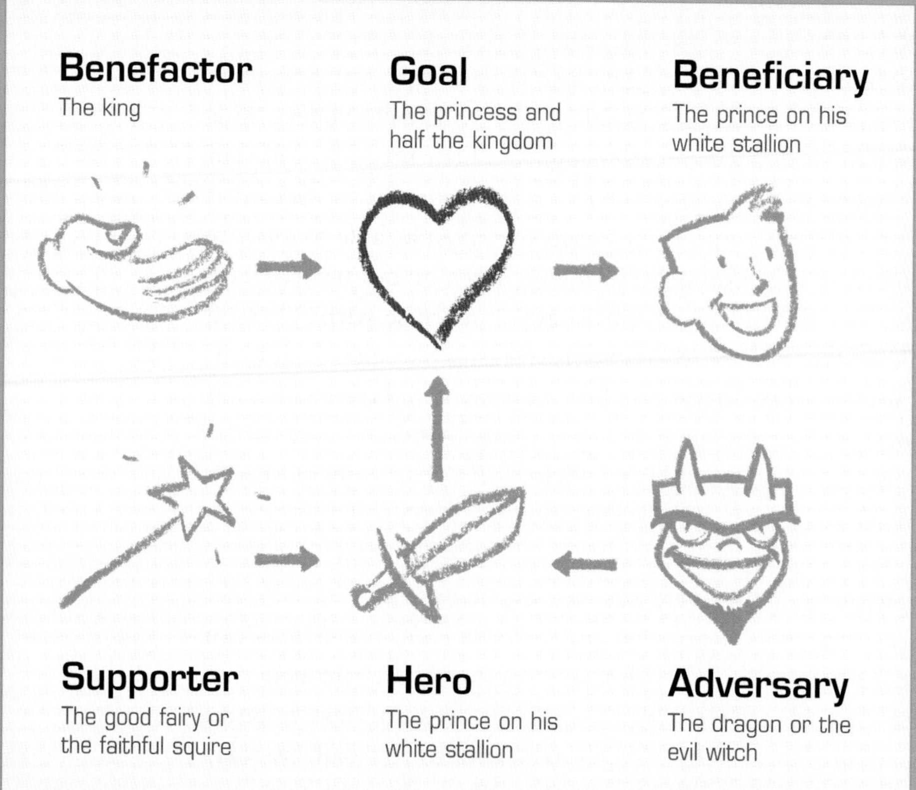

Benefactor
The king

Goal
The princess and half the kingdom

Beneficiary
The prince on his white stallion

Supporter
The good fairy or the faithful squire

Hero
The prince on his white stallion

Adversary
The dragon or the evil witch

Source: Inspired by Greimas (1974)

© 2004 SIGMA

Figure 2.5 outlines the relationship between the conflict, the cast of characters and the flow of events when telling a story. The Y-axis shows the tension curve and conflict development. The X-axis shows the timeline and the curve shows at what point the characters are usually introduced and how they influence the story.

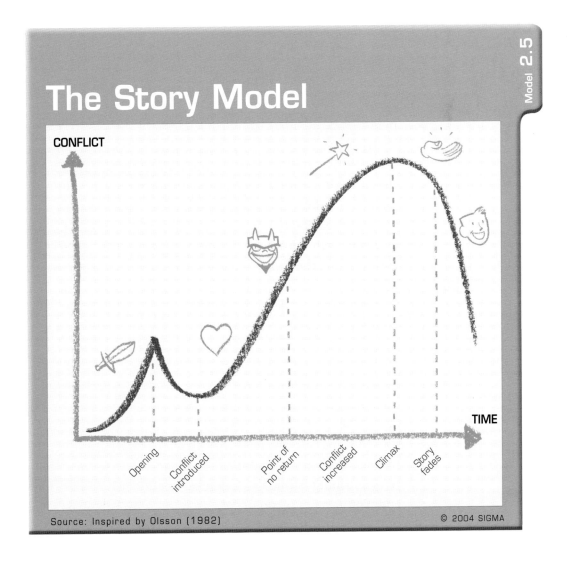

Model **2.5**

The Story Model

CONFLICT

TIME

Opening   Conflict introduced   Point of no return   Conflict increased   Climax   Story fades

Source: Inspired by Olsson (1982)

© 2004 SIGMA

Having discussed the four elements of storytelling, we are now ready to delve deeper into the relationship between branding and storytelling and shed light on how storytelling can be applied by companies.

Tell a Tale

Once the conflict and cast of characters are in place, you need to consider how the events and story will unfold. Try telling your story based on the following questions:

· How does the story *open*?
· How is the *conflict* introduced?
· What is the *point of no return* in the story?
· What is the *climax* of the story?
· How does the story *fade out* – how is the moral of the story presented?

Storytelling in Business 3

So how do companies go about using storytelling when it comes down to business?

In the following chapter, we will take a closer
look at storytelling both as a strategic branding concept, and as an operational communication tool.

In the last chapter we discussed the four elements of storytelling, outlining the process of putting a story together. The
following chapter shows how companies can use this process
for several purposes; both on a strategic management level, and
on an operational level in day-to-day communication with
employees.

Storytelling as a Branding Concept

As storytelling increasingly catches the eye of the business community, the mantra has become: companies must tell a story
that beats a path to the heart of the consumer. The best storytellers will be the winners of the future. But what does it
actually mean for companies to "tell a story"?

At the beginning of the book, we talked about how a strong
brand represents a story. Harley-Davidson for example represents the story of "freedom", while Nike, represents the "will to
win". In this way, storytelling becomes an effective tool for
creating an entire brand concept: one that stays with us,
because it touches our emotions.

*The story that is closely tied
into a company's corporate
brand, is the core story.*

The story that is closely tied into a company's corporate brand
is the *core story*. The core story expresses the fundamental

theme, or, the central nervous system that ties all the company's brand communication together: The silver thread, if you like. Nike's core story about the "will to win" therefore, means that all Nike's communication is structured on that one, common theme.

By analysing Nike's core story using the Fairy-tale Model (figure 3.1), we can see that it has both a clearly defined conflict and a strong cast of characters. Basically, it has all the elements necessary to make a good story.

By comparison the LEGO brand represents a story of "learning through creative play". Here, the goal is to encourage creative development in children. The heroes are LEGO Company employees, support comes in the form of LEGO bricks which stimulate creativity and imagination, and the adversaries are represented by passive entertainment, such as television.

A core story charts the course for the entire corporate brand. It should act as a compass directing all company communication both internally and externally. And it is precisely here that storytelling becomes a strategic tool for top management. Chapter 4 goes into more detail about how management can find and develop the core story of their company's corporate brand.

A core story charts the course for the entire corporate brand.

Corporate and Product Brands

Storytelling is useful both on a corporate and on a product level. The crucial factor being that the company keeps a firm eye on its long-term brand strategy.

Storytelling is useful both on a corporate and on a product level.

Within businesses there are a number of basic brand strategies. Nike and Procter & Gamble represent opposite poles of the spectrum. Nike's brand is a corporate brand that exists independently of the individual products, yet, these products e.g.

Nike Air, also support the overall Nike corporate brand; the essence of what makes Nike, Nike.

A range of strong product brands like Pampers and Pringles on the other hand, drives Procter & Gamble. These product brands exist independently within their own clearly defined identities, while corporate Procter & Gamble stays quietly in the background. For a company like this, the strategic challenge is to create strong core stories for each of its product brands in such a way that they do not conflict with each other, or with the corporate brand.

We will not go further into this discussion, however, all the evidence points to an increased focus on corporate brands and what they stand for. In part; this is due to the fact that companies can no longer hide behind corporate walls. The consumer is more switched on, and has more access to information via publications, television and the Internet than ever before. In turn, this information can be exchanged and discussed in a public domain leading to a far more transparent market place. Add to this heightened consumer awareness about ethical behaviour in the global market, and consumers are in a powerful position to make informed choices on the brands they buy into that transcend need and desire alone. Effectively, they are making a statement about their own set of beliefs. Companies therefore, need to offer brands that help the consumer navigate and make choices in the marketplace of tomorrow.

Storytelling as a Communication Tool

Along with its strategic value as a branding concept, storytelling can also be hugely effective in operational communication purposes. One example is when we use stories to communicate our purpose in a given context e.g. a simple anecdote that we share with our colleagues when explaining a point, or reinforcing an argument. Even the smallest anecdote contains the four key

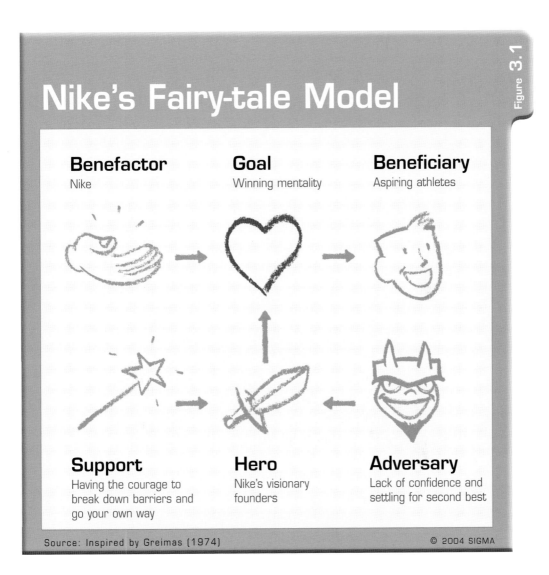

Nike's Fairy-tale Model

Benefactor
Nike

Goal
Winning mentality

Beneficiary
Aspiring athletes

Support
Having the courage to
break down barriers and
go your own way

Hero
Nike's visionary
founders

Adversary
Lack of confidence and
settling for second best

Source: Inspired by Greimas (1974)

© 2004 SIGMA

Figure 3.1

elements of storytelling and it easily travels by word of mouth.
Remember the story of the security guard who refused his boss
entry to his own company for not having valid ID?

Throughout the course of this book, we aim to show how companies can use storytelling as a dynamic communication tool
in a number of different situations, both internally and externally.

Figure 3.2

The Storytelling Pyramid

Storytelling as a Branding Concept

STRATEGIC LEVEL
The company's core story creates consistency in all company communications - internally as well as externally. As a branding concept storytelling can be applied on both corporate and product brand level.

Storytelling as a Communication Tool

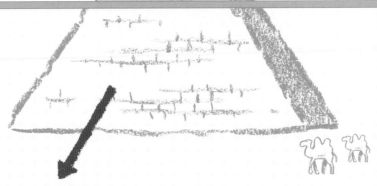

OPERATIONAL LEVEL
Stories and anecdotes can be used when communicating the company's message internally and externally. As a communication tool storytelling can be applied in a variety of contexts - e.g. in a presentation or a commercial.

The Company Core Story 4

In order to stay in the game, companies need to work with their brand as if it is a continually unfolding story. This chapter takes a closer look at how companies can use storytelling as a strategic branding tool and at how they can develop the core story of their brand.

"Once upon a time a man out on his morning stroll came upon three bricklayers busy at work. The man was curious to know what they were building and asked the first bricklayer what he was doing. The bricklayer replied irritably that he was busy laying bricks. What did it look like? Since this really gave the man no further insight into what they were building, he went on to ask the next bricklayer. The bricklayer gave him a quick glance and answered that he was busy building a wall. The man moved on and reached the third bricklayer who was whistling merrily. He decided to ask one last time. The bricklayer stopped working, mopped his brow and replied proudly: "I'm building the towns new cathedral".

This story shows how important it is to our motivation and self worth, to know that our efforts contribute to something with a deeper meaning. In a simplified way, it shows why it is so important for companies to have a core story: something that becomes a motivating beacon for employees, and ensures the company communicates a clear and consistent message.

Building a Foundation Starts From Within

For management, the first step in developing the company's core story is to create a shared mental image of the company's reason for being. This image needs to address both head and companies are usually fighting for an idea; e.g. Apple Computer fights to provide us with the means for creative expression through user-friendly digital technology. In the business world, it is not dragons and demons that stand in your way, but nevertheless, the adversary can take on many guises. It could be "diabolical" competitors, or it could be the companies themselves - those lacking the ability to innovate for example, or those battling against negative public opinion that must be swayed if they are to survive.

A company's quest in business, in many ways resembles the fairy-tale where the handsome prince rides off to rescue his damsel in distress and lives happily ever after.

Using the principles of storytelling helps a company to paint a picture of a challenge, or an "adversary", that employees need to overcome through teamwork, by applying their own unique skills, or through some kind of "heroism". It is well known that a shared challenge or enemy creates a stronger sense of togetherness. It reinforces the spirit and culture of the company, at the same time sending a clear message of what the company's values are to its wider surroundings.

By using a story as their strategic focal point, management has a more acute means of motivating employees, and letting the environment know exactly how their company makes a difference. The following example shows a strong core story that really was centred on a perilous quest.

NASA's Core Story

CASE

The United States space program embodied by NASA – the National Aeronautics and Space Administration – achieved dramatic results in the 1960s, thanks in no small part to the fact that NASA employees had a clear-cut and very compelling core story that they could all relate to. This change in outlook occurred during the early part of the decade, when President John F. Kennedy announced to the world that America would be the first nation to put a man on the Moon, and that they would do it before the end of the decade.

By introducing the possibility of sending a man to the Moon, President Kennedy created a strong, shared vision that made sense both to NASA employees as well as to the American public. It triggered dreams of achieving the impossible. Meanwhile, back at NASA the story captured the hearts and minds of employees, creating a shared value system based on innovation, creativity and no compromise. Values that were essential if this dream were ever to come true. Externally, Kennedy could justify significant increases in public spending on space exploration, and throughout the 1960s, the NASA brand became synonymous with the dream of journeying to the Moon.

Throughout the 1960s, the NASA brand became synonymous with the dream of journeying to the Moon.

Kennedy's story had a clear-cut conflict. There was no mistaking the identity of the adversary: the USSR and communism. And the hero? NASA of course – defender of democracy. The story also had a clearly defined message and a clearly defined goal that would require an extraordinarily heroic effort if it were to be achieved. In a race against the clock, the dream shared by President Kennedy fired up employees of NASA to bring out their strongest characteristics; steadfastness, creativity and above all courage. Many sacrificed their lives on this long and perilous quest. But in 1969 NASA achieved the impossible, as the first human being ever, Neil Armstrong, set foot on the Moon. The USA had won a mighty technological and ideological victory over the dragon from the USSR.

Regardless, in the years after this magnificent achievement, NASA's core story began losing the conflict on which it was built. The quest that NASA fought to achieve – to put a man on the Moon – had been accomplished. Pressure from the Russians had dissipated. Without communism to defeat, or the Moon to land on, NASA's purpose became clouded. And ever since the end of the Cold War, NASA has faced an increasing relevancy crisis. Space travel has become almost routine, and NASA has made no new breakthrough discoveries. New generations that

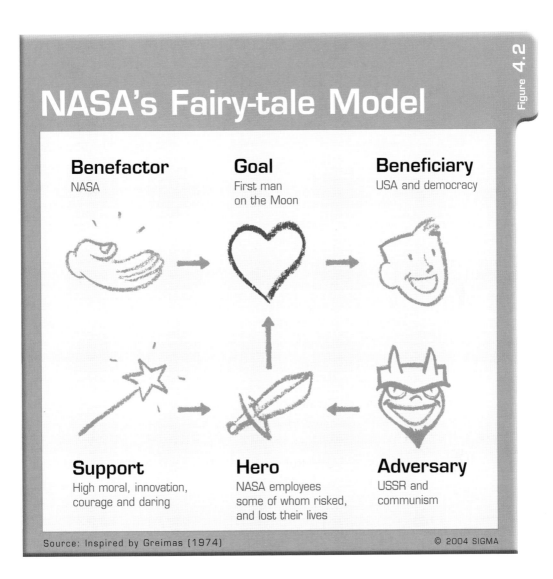

Figure 4.2

NASA's Fairy-tale Model

Benefactor
NASA

Goal
First man
on the Moon

Beneficiary
USA and democracy

Support
High moral, innovation,
courage and daring

Hero
NASA employees
some of whom risked,
and lost their lives

Adversary
USSR and
communism

Source: Inspired by Greimas (1974)   © 2004 SIGMA

never watched the Moon landings in 1969 are only vaguely aware of what the space programme actually does, apart from sending astronauts into orbit or making occasional fatal shuttle launches. Something indicates that it is time to reinvent this spellbinding story, at the same time revitalising the NASA brand both internally and externally: A story that clearly shows why NASA remains relevant now and in the future.

NASA may not be lost in space much longer, however. President Bush's announcement that the USA is determined to put a man on Mars has marked the beginning of what could be a new story for NASA to tell. The Mars adventure could make NASA's core story of the ultimate space exploration, relevant in the future – at least for the next 25 years. However, as we become increasingly desensitised to space travel, we will need bigger and brighter stories to fire our imaginations. Should NASA discover life in space for example, they will perhaps have hit on the biggest story of all time. ■

The case of NASA shows the strength in purposely thinking of brands in a captivating story context that embodies vision, mission and values.

The case of NASA shows the strength in purposely thinking of brands in a captivating story context that embodies vision, mission and values. But it also illustrates that a core story cannot last forever. There will be times where it is necessary to reinvent a company's core story in order for it to remain relevant for both employees and the surroundings.

From Values to Story

Seeing storytelling as a strategic tool triggers a natural evolution in the traditional thinking behind brands. When the classical branding concept is fused with the logic of storytelling, we move from perceiving a brand as a set of brand values to working with the brand as a living, core story.

Values in themselves are just words, devoid of any real content.

The explanation is simple. Values in themselves are just words, devoid of any real content. So when a company's values are presented as a list of bullet points in the Annual Report, at executive meetings or in an image brochure, they become anonymous and irrelevant, speaking to the mind but not to the heart. When you tell a story on the other hand, those terms come to life through powerful images and place your values in a more dynamic context. Bingo! Suddenly everyone knows and understands what you are trying to say, because you're giving them something that they can actually apply in daily life.

From Brand Values to Core Story

Using the logic of storytelling prompts a natural evolution in traditional branding concepts:

Brand Values
Values in themselves are little more than empty words. They speak only to reason.

Core Story
A story puts those values into perspective and into a human context. Those values then make sense and speak to both reason and emotions.

Model 4.3

© 2004 SIGMA

Figure 4.3 illustrates the development in the perception of brands. Effectively, a core story equals brand values transformed into a single, unifying and meaningful message. Basically, they are wrapped up in prettier, more easily digested packaging. It is unlikely that President Kennedy's message would have got the same results, had he just pushed NASA to work harder and left it to the American public to pay the bill. Instead he got people involved by capturing their imaginations, at the same time increasing motivation and spurring growth in the US economy.

The remainder of this chapter takes a closer look at how companies can start developing a strong core story for their brand, starting with a trip to the lab.

StoryLab: Developing the Company Core Story

Imagine yourself dressed in a white lab coat and protective glasses, surrounded by test tubes and sizzling flasks. You are

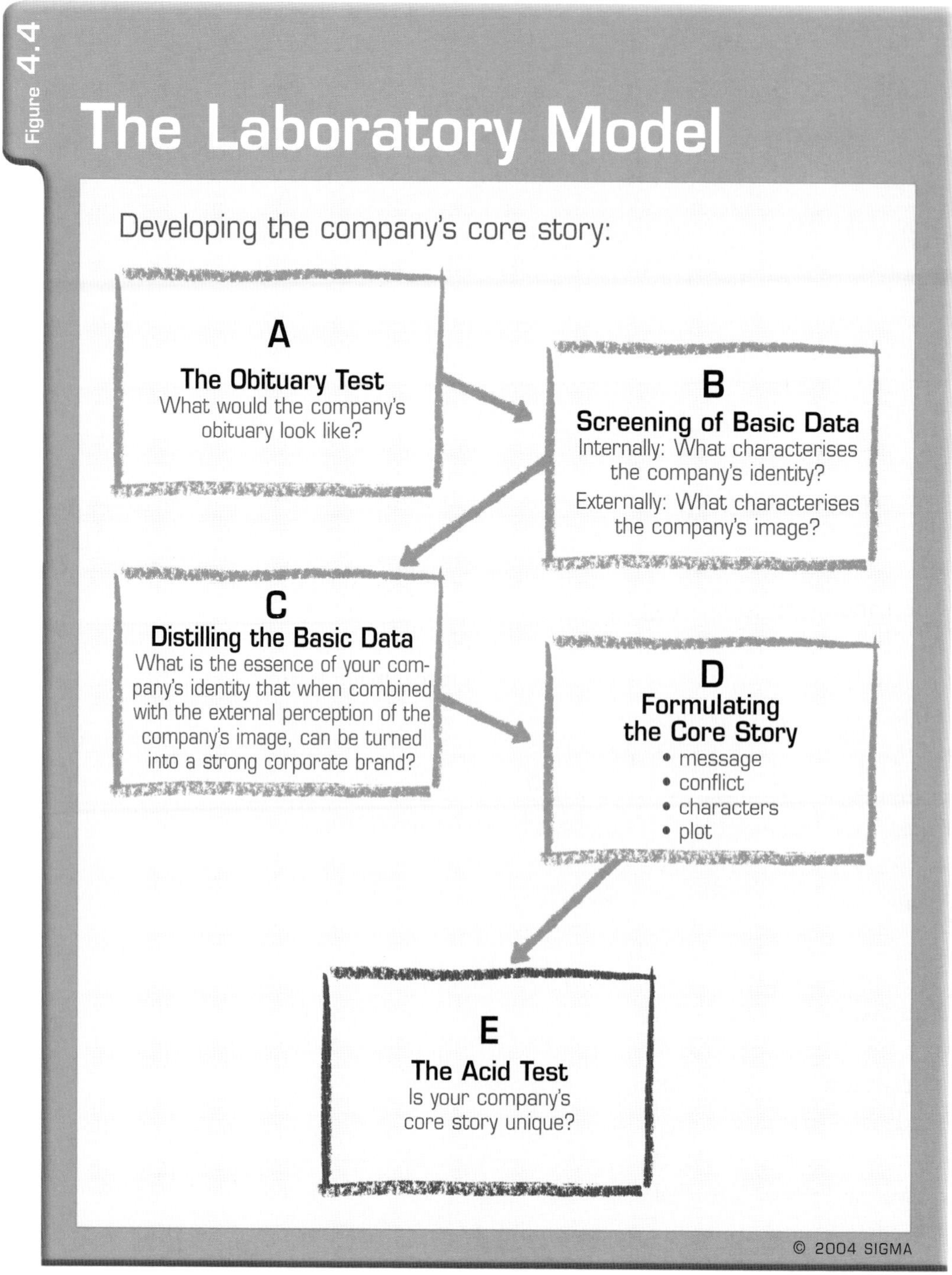

Figure 4.4

The Laboratory Model

Developing the company's core story:

A
The Obituary Test
What would the company's
obituary look like?

B
Screening of Basic Data
Internally: What characterises
the company's identity?
Externally: What characterises
the company's image?

C
Distilling the Basic Data
What is the essence of your company's identity that when combined
with the external perception of the
company's image, can be turned
into a strong corporate brand?

D
**Formulating
the Core Story**
• message
• conflict
• characters
• plot

E
The Acid Test
Is your company's
core story unique?

© 2004 SIGMA

in fact standing in the laboratory for storytelling: *StoryLab*. Armed with the four basic elements of storytelling, it is time to start experimenting with the core story of your company – the strategic communication platform for your company's brand. It must express your company's distinctive character. Why are you here? What are you fighting for? What would the world be like without you? In short, it is about finding out your company's reason for being.

It is about finding out your company's reason for being.

The experiments carried out in the StoryLab are intended to plant a seed that will grow into a strong basic framework – a tree trunk – for your company brand. With the four elements of storytelling, you already have some of the ingredients necessary to put you on to the right path. But first you have to do some solid groundwork.

The Laboratory Model (figure 4.4) illustrates the process of developing the company's core story, while the remainder of this chapter will discuss each step of the process in detail.

Would Your Company Be Missed?

It may sound morbid, but the Obituary Test is crucial in identifying and formulating the company's reason for being. This is precisely what the core story must express if it is to concisely communicate the company brand.

Most of us have had the unfortunate experience of being dumped by a lover. A classic case of not realising what you've got until it's gone. All too often, it is only when we have lost what we really cared about, that we realise what it was that made it so special. The Obituary Test is centred on this argument, forcing the company to take a long, hard look in the mirror and honestly consider what, if anything, would be missed should the company die.

Honestly consider what, if anything, would be missed should your company die.

It is not the most pleasant of tasks, granted, but the Obituary Test is the most effective means of starting the process.

It is worth keeping in mind the Obituary Test throughout the entire process of finding your core story. When push comes to shove, a strong brand is all about making a difference, and this will be your guiding reference point throughout your journey through StoryLab.

TEST

The Obituary Test

To begin:
Write down your company's obituary.

How would the obituary read if your customers were to write it?

How would the obituary read if your competitors were to write it?

Some useful questions:
What would the world look like if your company did not exist?

If your company were to close tomorrow, who would miss it? Why?

Has your company made any real difference for its stakeholders?

CASE

Coca-Cola's Real-life Obituary Test

Entirely by accident, the world's leading brand, Coca-Cola came very close to taking a real-life Obituary Test back in 1985, when it decided to change its original formula.

The early 1980s found Coke dangerously close to losing the cola war to Pepsi. In fact, Coke's market share in the US had been shrinking for decades, from 60% just after World War II to under 24% in 1983. Worse, carefully monitored blind taste tests showed that in more than half the cases, people preferred the taste of Pepsi. Coca-Cola's solution was to introduce a new secret formula coke that tasted smoother and sweeter than the original. More like Pepsi, in fact. The Coca-Cola Company spent 4-million US dollars on market research and tested it on 200,000 blind tasters. It was a winner. People liked the new Coke far better than either the original Coca-Cola or Pepsi.

On 23 April 1985, Coca-Cola introduced the new formula marking the first formula change in 99 years, at the same time ceasing production of the original formula. The "old Coke" was gone forever...

The reaction from consumers however, wasn't quite what Coke executives had expected. There was outrage. Consumers quite literally panicked, filling their basements with cases of original Coke. One man in San Antonio, Texas, drove to a local bottler and bought $1,000 worth of Coca-Cola. Calls flooded in to the 800-GET-COKE phone line, and to Coca-Cola offices across the United States. By June, the Coca-Cola Company was getting 1,500 calls a day on its consumer hotline, compared with 400 a day before the big announcement. People seemed to hold any Coca-Cola employee personally responsible for the change. Of course, the executives had to take their share of the beating. Coke CEO Roberto Goizueta received a letter addressed to "Chief Dodo, The Coca-Cola Company." Another angry customer wrote to him asking for his autograph because, in years to come, the signature of "one of the dumbest executives in American business history" would be worth a fortune.

Pepsi, naturally, jumped on the bandwagon and gave all their employees the day off to celebrate, on the premise that by changing their formula Coke had publicly admitted that it wasn't "the real thing". Around the country protest groups popped up with tag-names like "Society for the Preservation of the Real Thing" and "Old Cola Drinkers of America", which claimed to have 100,000 supporters, all of whom demanded the "old" Coke back. The Coca-Cola Company got the hint. On 11 July 1985 the "old" Coca-Cola formula was returned to store shelves as "Coca-Cola Classic". The story made the front page of virtually every major newspaper. The television network ABC even interrupted *General Hospital* to break the news. In just two days after the announcement, the Coca-Cola Company received 31,600 telephone calls on its Hotline. Anger melted into forgiveness, and then turned to celebration.

Looking back on this incident, one can't help wondering what on earth Coca-Cola were thinking about. To put it simply, they made the mistake of focusing only on the physical feature of the product – the taste – while completely ignoring the emotional attachment forged between the brand and the people. They had forgotten the fact that Coca-Cola had been an integral part of American life for more than a century. That it was part of the American identity. Coke was much more than a cola flavoured drink; it was an American institution – a national icon.

It took the loss of the beverage people had grown up with and fallen in love over, to remind them how much it meant to them. Gaye Mullins from Seattle, Washington and front man of the activist group Old Cola Drinkers of America said simply; "They can't do it. It's un-American. We've fought wars to have choice and freedom. I couldn't have been more upset if they'd burned the flag in my front yard". At a press conference announcing the return of the original formula Donald Keough (then the company's President and Chief Operating Officer) admitted: "The passion for original Coca-Cola — and that is the word for it, passion — was something that caught us by surprise. It is a wonderful American mystery, a lovely American enigma, and you cannot measure it any more than you can measure love,

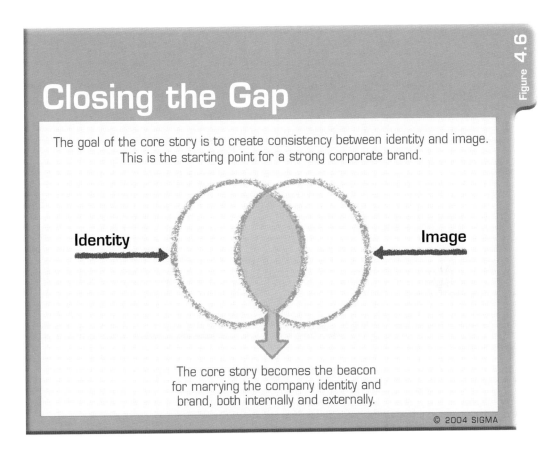

Closing the Gap

The goal of the core story is to create consistency between identity and image. This is the starting point for a strong corporate brand.

Identity   Image

The core story becomes the beacon for marrying the company identity and brand, both internally and externally.

Figure 4.6

problem boiling down to the fact that the company has failed to show how it makes a difference, or, adequately explain what values it holds. In cases such as these, by distilling your basic data, you can identify areas that should be emphasised in future communication in order to pull your identity and image together.

But the explanation for this gap may run far deeper, relating to substance or content e.g. when the company fails to deliver relevant or quality products or services to the consumer. In this case communication or storytelling can do little to help. This is a fundamental problem, demanding radical changes to the company's overall business plan.

However, once you know what the differences between identity and image are, you can start working on bringing the two areas closer together (figure 4.6).

The question of relevance for the company's stakeholders is a vital reference point when distilling internal and external basic data. Are there common denominators in what employees, customers, partners and opinion-leaders consider to be relevant in relation to the company? If you can identify and list three criteria of relevance, which transcend the various groups, then you are well on your way to narrowing your focus and building a strong foundation for your core story that unites your company's identity and public image in one, holistic brand.

At last, the process of formulating your core story can begin. Here it is helpful to experiment with the four elements of storytelling to ensure that your story complies with the basic rules of storytelling.

Formulating the Company Core Story

The hero in our fairy-tale ventures out in pursuit of happiness. Indiana Jones defies evil, Nazis and poisonous snakes in order to find the Holy Grail. NASA astronauts risked their lives to put a man on the Moon. What does your company fight for? What is its Holy Grail? If your company does not stand for something more profound than making money, then it probably does not make a memorable difference to employees or customers either.

The dynamics of a strong brand exist precisely because the company is constantly battling to overcome challenges and adversaries in order to achieve its cause.

The dynamics of a strong brand exist precisely because the company is constantly battling to overcome challenges and adversaries in order to achieve its cause. A "cause" does not necessarily mean that the company has to pursue an ideological quest, but it does mean that your company needs to make a difference in the business in which it operates. You need to think about what added value, experiences and dreams your customers buy into as well as the actual product or service your company offers. Basically, what kind of a story does your customer take part in? Before you move on, try putting the book down for a few minutes and answer the following question concisely:

How does your company make a difference?

It can be difficult to give a short, simple answer. But it has to be simple. Supposing you are the person who knows your company best, if you cannot give a simple answer, then how can anyone else? Your first challenge is to sum up your company's core story in one sentence. Let us start the process by going through the four elements of storytelling one by one.

If you cannot give a simple answer, then how can anyone else?

Your Message

Your message should not be confused with a pay-off or a slogan. A pay-off is a short, catchy expression that encompasses the message typically used in company advertising. For example "Just Do It" is Nike's pay-off, however their message is that every game is about winning, and if you want it badly enough, with effort and determination, you can be a winner too.

But what Nike is fighting for, is to help us believe in ourselves. If we believe in ourselves, throw caution to the wind and just go for it, then we can all be winners. Nike is fighting against compromise and the seeds of defeat that lie in our lack of confidence and our tendency to settle for second best. Nike says; if we want to be the best we need to go all the way. During the Olympic Games in Atlanta in 1996, the whole city saw large billboards go up, all expressing a message in sharp contrast to Olympic ideals: "You don't win silver, you loose gold".

Likewise, when Anita Roddick founded The Body Shop back in 1976, she created a hard-hitting message to go with it. The company, and by association both employees and customers, stood for something important. Besides fighting for a number of political and charitable causes, The Body Shop took a stand against animal testing, a taboo that had plagued the cosmetics industry for years. By contrast, in The Body Shop universe, cosmetics and skincare are a guilt-free experience. It is our decision whether we are willing to suffer for beauty or not, but animals need not suffer.

The message in the company core story is the moral of the story. It is a company's sense on what is right and wrong.

To stay in storytelling jargon, you could say that the message in the company core story is the moral of the story. Basically, it is a company's sense of what is right and wrong. For Volvo the most important thing is not to get there fast, but to get there safely. Volvo buyers first and foremost buy into a story about safety. It is the same story that Volvo employees stand by when they strive to develop stronger, safer cars that can handle even the toughest crash test. The same is true for Alfa Romeo, though their message is quite different to that of Volvo. The essence of Alfa Romeo's message is one of driving pleasure. A passion that is as much about enjoying the journey as it is about getting there. In the Alfa Romeo universe, driving is one of life's great leisure pursuits, and it doesn't hurt to look the part while you are doing it.

In essence, your message needs to mirror either your cause, or, the experience you are trying to sell. For renowned Danish shipping company A.P. Moller - Maersk Group, the central message has always been that discipline, punctuality and thoroughness is the foundation of a sound business. In return, their customers can be safe in the knowledge that things are always in order. The founder of the company used to express his message in two words "punctual perfection", a term that to this day, is firmly rooted at the heart of the company and its core story.

The Classical Hero

Greek mythology is the scene for an astonishing array of classical heroes. Homer's classic, *The Iliad*, recounts the Greeks' yearlong war against Troy. His heroes are out in full force and in all their glory. Hercules, son of the god Zeus takes on the role of the brave and valiant *hero*. He is the strongest and most fearless of all the Greeks, and can solve the most impossible of tasks. Odysseus is the *adventurer*, who on his ten-year long journey home from Troy encounters all kinds of imaginable and unimaginable challenges, including an encounter with the one eyed Cyclops. The Greek commander Agamemnon is your archetypical *ruler* who single-mindedly charges ahead dominating his surroundings. Achilles on the other hand, is the archetypical *rebel*. In the story, Achilles dares to defy the great Agamemnon, challenging his ruling power by following the beat of his own drum. Among the Greeks, Nestor represents the *wise* hero. In Greek mythology age and wisdom are often one and the same, and Nestor is the oldest of the wise men. When he speaks every-body listens. Even the most powerful commanders dare not object. The greatest of the Trojan heroes, Hector – slain by Odysseus – is portrayed as the *caring* hero. Before going off to war he says an emotional goodbye to his family and comforts his weeping child. Another Trojan, Paris, takes the role of the archetypical *lover*. A hot-blooded and seductive warrior, he abducts the fair Helena and marries her, despite the fact that he is already married to another.

The point is each hero has a strong set of personal skills and character traits. Each represents a set of values and is driven by his passion. Some seek freedom, rebellion or adventure; others seek love, caring and acknowledgement. The classical hero figure thus appeals to very basic wants and needs that are deeply embedded in human nature. It is no wonder that the hero figures of ancient Greece are still alive and well in today's world. Just take a look at the entertainment industry. Here the adventurer

Each hero represents a set of values and is driven by his passion.

Figure 4.9

Outline of the Classical Heroes

Hero figures	Characteristics	Goal	Opponent
The Brave Hero i.e. Nike and Red Cross	Brave and headstrong with a firm belief in him/her self	Fighting for a better world - believing every-one can be a winner	Fear, weakness, and evil at large
The Lover i.e. Alfa Romeo and Antonio Banderas	Hot-blooded and sensual	Following your heart - satisfying your emotional needs	Reason, or lack of passion
The Adventurer i.e. Virgin and Indiana Jones	Curiosity and daring	Exploring the world, journeying into new territory	Narrow-mindedness and the constraints of daily life
The Creator i.e. the LEGO Company and Steven Spielberg	Imagination and creativity	To create and develop new ways of expressing oneself	Repetition and passiveness
The Joker i.e. M&M and Jim Carrey	Humour and joyfulness	To entertain others and enjoy life	Boredom
The Innocent i.e. Disney and Meg Ryan	Honesty, innocence and a big heart	To uphold truth and justice	To do wrong
The Magician i.e. 3M and Harry Potter	Full of ideas and surprising	Making dreams come true and showing that nothing is impossible	Stagnation, or, lack of control
The Rebel i.e. Harley-Davidson and Jack Nicholson	Rebellious and uncompromising	Going against the grain and breaking the rules	The system and dominating norms
The Ruler i.e. Mercedes and Bill Gates	Ability to lead, authority and class	Gaining control, security and order	Rebellion and disorder
Everyday Hero i.e. John Goodman and People magazine	Earthbound and straight forward	To find tranquillity in being part of the community	Lack of acceptance by your surroundings
The Caregiver i.e. Volvo and Mother Teresa	Caring and giving	To support and help other people	Selfishness
The Wise Hero i.e. Barnes & Noble and Albert Einstein	Intelligence and expertise	The search for truth and exploring life's great mysteries.	Ignorance and lies

Source: Inspired by Pearson & Mark (2001)

© 2004 SIGMA

e.g. Harrison Ford, the lover e.g. Antonio Banderas, and the rebel e.g. Jack Nicholson are used time and again in slight variations on the same theme. Figure 4.9 outlines the most common hero profiles and clarifies the type of hero the company becomes in its core story. By using these profiles as a point of reference, your company has an alternative tool for describing its values. The hero figure literally adds flesh and bones to the company's role in the story universe. At the same time, it also sheds light on the conflict and the passion that drives the brand forward.

The hero figure literally adds flesh and bones to the company's role in the story universe.

For companies, the challenge is to place itself within just one of these hero profiles, though some of these frameworks do overlap. For example, your hero can be both rebel and adventurer. Richard Branson and his company Virgin are a great mix of an adventurer and a rebel. The important thing, is to narrow down your selection, and stick with the hero figure you identify within your company. It also helps to consider "the hero" from the customer's perspective. Will your customer be able to identify with the personality of the hero? Are your hero and customer searching for the same thing – be it adventure or rebellion?

Your Plot

With your message, conflict and cast of characters in place, it is time to put the final element, the plot, in place. Because a company's core story is a strategic platform for communication, it must be presented in a way that can be translated to actual stories in many different contexts. It is difficult, therefore to speak of plot, as such. Nevertheless, it can be a good internal exercise to try and tell the core story as a fairy-tale, simply to see if it works in accordance with the principles of storytelling. By telling your core story in this way, your company is placed in a sequence of events that can be easily understood.

It can be a good internal exercise to try and tell the company's core story as a fairy-tale.

The management team of SuperBest, a chain of Danish super-markets used this technique at their annual convention in 2002 for presenting their strategy to their 170 stores.

CASE

The Fairy-tale of Independent Grocers

SuperBest is a chain of Danish supermarkets made up of independent grocers. This basically means that the individual grocer enjoys the privilege of being their own boss and owning their own stores, while under the protective umbrella of SuperBest. By working together in a chain structure, these grocers gain scale benefits in purchasing and have the opportunity to take part in national marketing under one joint name. The business advantages are one thing. But one of the SuperBest chain's continuing challenges is to narrow down and visualise the value-base, tying together 170 individual and ultimately different grocers. What do they actually have in common? And do they make a difference in relation to other, bigger supermarket chains that have everything the modern consumer wants? Supermarket giants are built on a tight, standardised concept. SuperBest grocers on the other hand, have the personal touch. They take personal pride in how their stores look, and what goods they sell. They chat with their customers on a daily basis and adapt their stores to local needs. It is precisely through this personal and localised experience, that SuperBest can make a difference. Good deals and quality products by contrast, are simply basic preconditions for running a modern supermarket.

In order to communicate this message to the 170 grocers at the annual strategy convention in 2002, the management team of the chain office decided to convey the message through a fairy-tale, with the purpose of creating a shared image of the grocery's basic values. The story went like this:

"Once upon a time the grocer was a man we all knew. He was always there with a friendly ear, a good deal, and some timely advice. He did not need a microscope to know good quality from bad, and he did everything in his power to create a store that his customers were comfortable in. The grocery was a gathering place for local people: the heart of the village.

But one day, everything changed. Large supermarkets moved like a dark shadow across the land of groceries. Economies of scale, effectiveness and unification were the new supermarkets' version of the grocer. They all looked alike: one, large grey concrete box. Customers became little more than a barcode at the cash register. And the virtues of a true grocer turned to dust in the back room. The personal touch was in short supply.

But genuine grocers lived on. Determined to safeguard and uphold a warm, personal and quality shopping experience, they formed a united front against the large, grey supermarkets. Respecting the diversity of their customers they held their heads up high under the parole, "Liberty, equality and good grocering!" Liberty: because they were free grocers, each of whom put their own individual touch onto their stores. Equality: because they had a clear and shared belief in providing quality customer service and good deals. And good grocering: because they hailed the true grocer virtues and knew that satisfied customers always come back.

The revolution had begun..."

SuperBest's core story is about the personal grocer who places the needs of their local customers first. It is these old-fashioned grocer values and the personal service that tie the many individual grocers together. ■

If Your Company Was a Fairy-tale....

What kind of fairy-tale would it be? Can you find a classic fairy-tale that is similar to the core story your company would like to represent? The advantage of using well-known fairy-tales is that we can all relate to them. Here are a few examples:

David and Goliath:
The Company is small and flimsy compared to its competitors, but thanks to determination and effort, it is able to challenge the big boys and emerge victorious – against all the odds.

The Hare and the Tortoise:
Rather than mindlessly following every new trend, the Company prefers to follow a tried and tested course one step at a time – the results will follow.

Denis the Menace:
The Company is characterised by its unconventional and capricious approach that sometimes shocks, often surprises but never, ever bores its customers. The Company is well liked because it acts honestly and with good intentions, without being fuddy-duddy.

Robin Hood:
The Company fights for justice. Even though it is relatively obscure itself, it is not afraid to battle against the dominating forces in the market. Forces that have created a monopoly, which do not benefit the consumer.

The Ugly Duckling:
The Company that started out as the black sheep that nobody thought would ever amount to anything. Regardless, with unwavering belief in its qualities and skills, it has become a force to be reckoned with, surprising and impressing even its harshest of critics.

The Acid Test

Having developed your core story – a clear formulation with a strong message, conflict and a clear cast of characters – we face the final and decisive test: The Acid Test.

The Acid Test determines whether the company's core story is unique in relation to its competitors. If we picture ourselves standing on a hilltop, overlooking the world of brands, closer inspection will reveal that a large number of companies are basically the same, representing the same core story with only very slight variations in packaging. What is the difference between Thomas Cook and Lunn Poly? Like most charter companies they are built on a story of families sharing good times together in the sun without a care in the world.

The Acid Test determines whether the company's core story is unique in relation to its competitors.

If your company decides to communicate a core story that looks just like the one being told by your competitors, it should only be on the basis that you have a better and more credible way of communicating that particular story. A core story should leave room for interpretation when it is translated into actual stories and campaigns. Therefore, companies often compete for ownership of the same core story. Think about the many credit card companies including American Express and Diners Club who compete for ownership of the story about "the ultimate individual freedom to do whatever you want, whenever you want it."

With the Acid Test, we're talking make or break time. All your competitors core stories and communication must be included in the comparison. If the core story your company has developed turns out to be too generic, you need to take another trip through *StoryLab*.

Authentic Raw Material for Storytelling 5

All companies have authentic raw material for telling their own stories: genuine, real-life episodes that can be used in the continuous communication of their brand. This chapter shows you where you can find them, and how you can use them as a concrete communication tool.

Once your company's core story has been identified and developed, you have created a strategic storytelling platform for your brand; a compass for all internal and external communication. Every time the company initiates a new communication initiative you need to ask: does this story come together as a chapter in our core story? The better the company is at ensuring even the smallest story supports the core story, the stronger and more consistent your brand will be.

The core story must be transformed into a collection of concrete stories.

In short, the core story must be transformed into a collection of concrete stories, which are relevant for your employees, customers and your surroundings. These concrete stories translate the core story into a language that makes it accessible and relevant to your company's stakeholders in a variety of contexts.

All Companies Have a Story to Tell

There is really no reason to invent stories to communicate your company's message if you already have all the stories about your company you need. These genuine stories add credibility to your message, and often they are far stronger than fictitious stories. Everyday stories spread through your organisation like a living organism, providing you with the raw material necessary for good storytelling. Just think of all the small anecdotes you could find in your daily working life, regardless of whether the sign on the door reads "The Coca-Cola Company", or "Backwater Office Supplies". It's all a question of knowing where to look, and knowing what your starting point is. You need to be clear about what these stories need to say before you start looking. At the same time, you need to be aware of the fact that storytelling is a dynamic and continuous process. First, the stories have to be identified and collected. Then they must be sorted and processed. Finally, they need to be communicated in the right way and in the right context.

Everyday stories spread through your organisation like a living organism, providing you with the raw material necessary for good storytelling.

Figure 5.1 illustrates the sources and places that are most likely to contain the raw material needed for storytelling.

Within the company itself, you will find an abundance of stories from the simple day-to-day running of the business. It can be difficult to spot these stories because you live them on a daily basis without being aware of their existence. But these little anecdotes, seemingly insignificant at first sight, may very well be the stories that most effectively show why your company is special.

Let us take a closer look at each of the areas in the model.

Employee Stories

Most company stories are about the values and culture that naturally spring from the heart of your company: your employees. These are the people who embody your company values on a daily basis. Equally, "rank" or the position of the individual employee is unimportant. A good story can be found with anybody; the receptionist, the product developer or the bookkeeper. Digging up stories is detective work. It requires research, patience and most importantly trust.

The employees are the people who embody your company values on a daily basis.

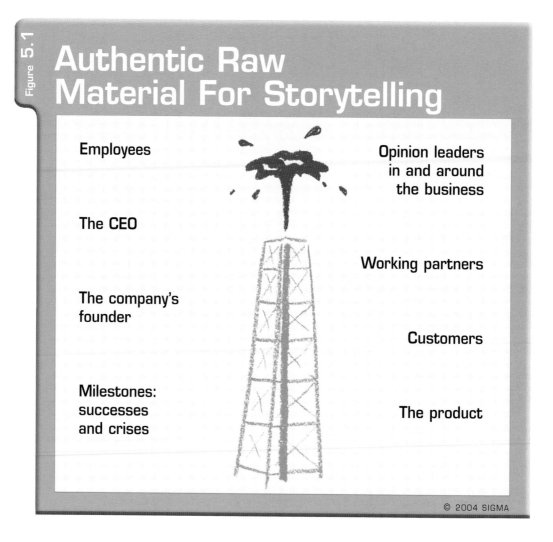

Figure 5.1

Authentic Raw Material For Storytelling

Employees

The CEO

The company's founder

Milestones: successes and crises

Opinion leaders in and around the business

Working partners

Customers

The product

© 2004 SIGMA

Here are a few tips and tricks:

- Begin by interviewing employees that you already know to be great ambassadors for the company i.e. those people who best represent the company's values. Start with employees who have a natural gift for telling stories and who like to do so.
- Ask about their experiences within the company, good and bad. Which stories do they tell their friends or colleagues? And what stories do their colleagues tell them?

- Are there individual accomplishments where an employee has stood out, or made a difference – either socially or professionally? This can also be a good lead into other stories.
- Be prepared to get new leads during the process. You will often hear bits and pieces of stories, where you will need to find the original source in order to get the full picture.
- Always consider what the stories say about your company values.

Nothing is Too Much Trouble

Comwell is a Scandinavian hotel chain where providing exceptional service is the very core of the business. The company core story is about the calibre of employees who will overcome any obstacle to make a guest happy. Comwell has put together a small folder called "All For You". In it, a number of employees recount personal experiences where they made an extra special effort to make their customers happy. A female secretary at Comwell, Denmark tells the following story:

CASE

"It was Midsummer's Eve and we were hosting a large wedding between a Danish bride and an American groom, at Comwell. The wedding party comprised 70 people who were invited to take part in traditionally Danish, Midsummer's Eve bonfire festivities on the beach close to the hotel. Unfortunately, that summer the fire department and the harbourmaster had put a ban on all private bonfires on the beach. The bride was in tears. She had desperately wanted her new husband and their guests from America to experience the festival. That same evening my husband and I had been invited to spend the evening with some close friends of ours, Ulla and Carsten. They had collected plenty of firewood for a huge bonfire in the garden of their home in the country. It occurred to me to give them a call. Happily, they had no objections if we brought along some extra guests. They had plenty of room in the garden, so seventy-four instead of four posed no problem. And this is how the bride got her groom and her traditional Danish Midsummer's Eve with bonfire, speeches and song." ■

Stories About the CEO

Stories about the CEO - both negative and positive - are told again and again in the company.

As the front man or woman of a company, the CEO has a symbolic significance in any business as their actions are observed and analysed by the employees and the surroundings. Stories about the CEO – both negative and positive – are told again and again within a company. Sometimes those stories circulate for so many years that it becomes unclear whether the story is real, or mythical. Regardless, the symbolic meaning remains the same.

Former CEO of Hewlet-Packard, Bill Hewlett, was a leader who understood the symbolic value of his actions and of the stories being told about him. One of the classical stories told about his management style goes as follows:

"Many years ago, Bill Hewlett was wandering around the Research & Development department and found the door to the storage room locked. He immediately cut the lock with a bolt-cutter and put a note on the door, 'Never lock this door again. Bill'. "

It is a story about trusting and respecting your employees. To Bill Hewlett, the locked door was a breach of these values and his actions sent a clear message to his employees. That story is still being told today.

A few tips on how to dig for stories about the CEO:
- Most stories about the CEO are to be found among employees. Start with the employees who work with the CEO on a daily basis.
- Consider if there are any "grapevine-stories" about the CEO? Find out what they are, and get them verified.

- Are there particular actions or rituals that the CEO is well known for?
- Has the CEO been involved in any major successes, or has he helped the company through crisis and tough times. How did he or she do it?
- Consider what the stories tell you about management style and the company values.

The Big Bang:
Stories About the Founding of the Company

The story of "how it all began" is part of every company's history. Indeed, many of these "founder-stories" are very similar. Who does not recognise the story of the two young up-starts who started what became a globally successful company from their parent's garage. Many of the dot.coms that shot to success during the 1990s and grew to record size in no time were founded in a garage or an attic somewhere in the small hours of the morning.

The story of "how it all began" is part of every company's history.

Another variation of the "founder-story" is the "geek-in-the-garage-story". This is the story of the ingenious engineer who built his company on a unique product, which he developed in his hobby-room. At Danfoss one of the largest manufacturers of thermostats and water pumps in the world, the story of the founder Mads Clausen is well known. Aged just 17, back in 1923, Mads filed the first patent for an invention of his and earned the nickname "Mads Patent". Ten years later, in 1933 Mads founded Danfoss. The story supports and reflects the company's core story of maintaining a "pioneering spirit of innovation"; values on which the company was built, and still rests on today.

Founder stories are variations on the same theme. Compaq (now merged with Hewlett-Packard) was founded by a group of IBM employees who had grown tired of working in a big, streamlined corporation. One day, during their lunch break they were sketching out ideas on a napkin and the idea for the laptop computer was born. They quit that same day and founded Compaq. Another example is that of the Hard Rock Café, which was founded by two Americans who were deeply frustrated by the fact that they could not get a decent burger in London. They started a burger restaurant where Eric Clapton became a regular. The fanfare for what would become a worldwide success story came the day that Clapton donated a signed guitar to the restaurant, and laid the foundation for the Hard Rock Café concept as we know it today.

Stories about the first tentative footsteps of companies all over the world often touch on the core values and mindset on which the companies rest.

Stories about the first tentative footsteps of companies all over the world often touch on the core values and mindset on which the companies rest. And often you will find the founder was driven by passion and the will to make a difference. It is often said that you are better equipped to face the future if you know your past. Knowing your roots gives you a feeling of identity. It provides ballast when decisions have to be made on the future of the company. Internally, the story of the company's founding has great importance for the identity of the employees. However, management within the company also needs to consider whether the story remains relevant to the company, today and in the future. Developments may have made changes in a way that means the "founder-story" no longer supports the core story.

A few tips for finding stories on the company's founding:
- Start by reading all available material on the company's history and development.
- Interview the founder if he or she is still with the company. Or, talk to senior employees who may have been there since the beginning.
- Ask what triggered the foundation of the company and how it happened?

shoe company far, far away! His shoes must have meant quite a lot to him. You don't get a story like this unless your company has truly earned it.

Sadly, most customer "love letters" tend to end up in an archive in customer services or in a secretary's desk drawer without anybody ever seeing them. However, one shouldn't underestimate the power of such a story. It could be valuable ammunition for the sales force when facing new customers. And it could boost the company spirit, making employees feel that they actually do make a difference.

Stories From Opinion Leaders

In the 1950s the sex symbol of sex symbols, Marilyn Monroe was famously asked what she wore to bed. Her answer went something like this, "Two drops of Chanel No.5 and nothing else...". Marilyn's racy reply not only triggered the imagination of her male admirers, it also gave a huge boost to Chanel who could now tell the story of Marilyn's preferred bedtime attire. The story was so powerful that Chanel No.5 still lives on the power of the icon and myth of Marilyn Monroe. It emphasises their story of femininity, eroticism and seduction.

An opinion leader is a person, an organisation or a cause that sets the agenda in a given field; for example, Marilyn Monroe was a role model for fashion, beauty and youth. The idea behind digging up stories from external opinion leaders all adds to your credibility when someone who knows what they are talking about recommends your company. The story told by opinion leaders may not be as rosy as if you were to tell it yourself, but the added credibility gives the story far more punch than you ever could have.

The story told by opinion leaders may not be as rosy as if you were to tell it yourself, but the added credibility gives the story far more punch than you ever could have.

An opinion leader does not necessarily have to be known. It could also be professionals or experts within a narrow field who are not immediately associated with the company. When the company "explains itself" through people from different worlds, whole new perspectives of looking at the brand often appear. Sourcing stories from opinion leaders requires thorough research and legwork, and it may be a good idea to proactively seek to establish a dialogue with opinion leaders either in or outside of the field of business: opinion leaders who may share an interest in the field in which the company operates, or who hold similar values to the company.

A few tips on digging up stories among opinion leaders:
- You should have a clear idea of the message that the opinion leader can contribute beforehand
- Identify the persons who set the agenda in the company's field of business. They will often be the preferred reference points of the media when they need a statement
- Consider if there are opinion leaders from other fields who may have an alternative approach to the company, or the company's product?
- Professional experts must not receive payment from your company. This would undermine their credibility. They need to have a professional shared interest in the company or its product, which in turn becomes the basis for opening up a dialogue. Of course, this means that the company must have the substance or profile that makes it interesting for the opinion leader to get involved in telling the company story in the first place.

CASE

Building Blocks for Life

The core story of the LEGO brand is about "learning through creative play". It is also the story told by people all over the world who have had good experiences with LEGO products. At www.lego.com and in the company's brand-book you can find the following story:

"A Canadian DNA-scientist was approached by a local television station that asked if he would appear in a program and explain to viewers what DNA is, and how it is structured. Naturally the scientist was delighted to take part in the program. The only question was how he was going to explain the complex structure of DNA, so that people – even a child – would understand what he was talking about. He had been contemplating this problem for a few days when he found some of his old LEGO bricks in his basement. This was it – the solution to his problem! By building a model of LEGO bricks in various colours he could clearly illustrate and explain the complex DNA structure in a way that everyone could understand. It worked so well that his DNA model of LEGO bricks was later used in a program on the Discovery Channel."

Even though the DNA scientist is not well known or famous, his professional expertise adds credibility. This simple anecdote emphasises that LEGO represents a universal language, and through the unlikely use of LEGO bricks by a DNA scientist, the product was placed in a new context that supported the brand values.

A Few Rules of Thumb

The various sources for finding your stories, underline the fact that in any company there is abundant raw material for storytelling. But as your research goes on, you will find it is rare to find these stories presented to you on a silver platter. Often, there are lots of fragments and bit-meal pieces of information that need to be processed before they can be shaped into a story.

The following are a few rules of thumb as to what to look for when gathering stories and processing the raw material into actual stories:

A good example

People have a tendency to speak in general terms. "It was a good period" or "We are more innovative than our competitors". Make them be specific. Have them tell stories of specific incidents, events or situations that express the sentiment.

The more concrete the better

Put faces on the characters in your story. What was said? How did they react? What was the mood?

A good story "speaks in images"

If you do not see images in your mind when hearing a story it is not concrete enough. Be sure to get the visual details.

Numbers are boring

Numbers and facts may be very important, but on their own they rarely make for a good story. They must be placed in a context.

Storytelling and history are not the same

"The company was founded in 1899 by a man in Liverpool" is not a good story in itself, but it may very well be the seed for a story.

The StoryDrivers of the Company

In the systematic process of extracting the raw material for storytelling, some hidden and untold stories about the company are likely to be revealed. It is also likely that you will encounter one or more areas that hold a larger concentration of stories, which express the company's core story. Gluts such as this are "StoryDrivers".

A StoryDriver helps express the company core story by making it relevant for the right people.

A StoryDriver helps express the company core story by making it relevant for the right people. The 3M Company is known for its ability to innovate and develop new products. As a brand it is built on the core story of "innovation at any cost". The core story is brought to life by the many internal stories of how new and groundbreaking products come to life in a unique culture of innovation. It is those stories about product development that constitute the central StoryDriver of 3M, helping to attract new employees and continuously strengthen the culture.

A charismatic and visionary leader who, through his actions becomes an icon for the company's story may also be a Story-Driver. Richard Branson and everything he represents is the central StoryDriver in the story of Virgin – the adventurous rebel who breaks with convention.

The choice of StoryDriver is a strategic decision. It should be grounded in an assessment of what stories best communicate the company's core story. Your authentic stories may not be equally applicable in all situations. Maybe they do not offer a forward-looking perspective on the core story, or maybe they are simply not relevant to some of the company's core target groups; some stories will be more relevant for customers than employees, and vice versa.

Sometimes inventing new stories, or staging some of its stories better serves the company. At Nike it was never authentic raw material that Michael Jordan and all the other star athletes wear Nike shoes. In order to express the core story externally, Nike has paid for this raw material and made it the central Story-Driver in their communication with customers. It works for Nike. But it is also a costly solution that only a few companies can afford. And it is not always credible to buy your stories. In any case, your genuine stories can be used as a starting point, or serve as inspiration for creating or inventing different stories.

Figure 5.2 illustrates the process of finding the company's StoryDrivers.

Figure 5.2

The Company's StoryDrivers

Your choice of StoryDriver centres on finding the focus areas of stories best suited strategically to communicating the company's core story.

Having extracted the authentic raw material for storytelling, we can usually identify one or more areas that hold a larger concentration of stories. With this starting point, we need to ask whether these stories are relevant for the target groups of the company? And do the stories support the company's core story?

StoryDriver

3. For which core target groups do the stories have particular relevance?

2. What areas hold the largest concentration of stories expressing the company's core story?

1. Collecting the necessary raw material.

© 2004 SIGMA

Storytelling as a Management Tool 6

If your company's employees cannot explain how you make a difference, then it is naive to think that customers should choose your company over your competitors. A strong brand stems from its employees; people who have to be strong ambassadors for the brand on a daily basis. In this chapter we discuss how storytelling can be used as a tool to strengthen the brand from within.

The stories we share with others are the building blocks of any human relationship. Stories place words and images on our shared experiences. They help shape our perception of "who we are" and "what we stand for". Likewise, stories are told and flow through all companies. By analysing and interpreting those stories we can uncover the organisations' values, making storytelling an important tool in the internal branding process. Likewise, through these stories, employees come to understand themselves and the company brand. And in turn, these stories help employees understand the reasoning behind the company's values and guide them towards actually living those brand values in day-to-day operations.

Through stories, employees come to understand themselves and the company brand.

Storytelling works as a supplement to traditional management tools. For managers, the task is to use storytelling to anchor the company's values, visions and culture within the organisation. As such, the goal should be to identify those stories, which best communicate the company's core story, at the same time ensuring that they will be told again and again. This is a continuous and organic process meaning that stories must be identified, developed and communicated on an ongoing basis if they are to get their messages across in a timely and relevant way.

There are two purposes for using storytelling as a management tool:

To strengthen the culture
· Translating the company's values in tangible ways that employees can easily understand.

To show the way
· Showing employees how they should behave in certain situations in order to uphold company values.

The following pages give concrete examples on how companies have used storytelling to achieve these purposes.

Building Blocks for a Strong Company Culture

Managers are often fond of fancy words, listing their carefully considered corporate values on any occasion they get; through the company newsletter, on bulletin boards, in the annual report or on the company website. They sound great, but in terms of actual value creation they are practically meaningless: little more than empty shells devoid of any real content. Typically, they look much like the value list of any other company. By explaining company values through stories however, those abstract values become tangible. The complex becomes concrete. Take 3M for example. Here is one company where storytelling has become an integrated part of the culture. Through stories told about their many inventors and pioneers, 3M and its many employees define what the company stands for, and by actively seeking and using a certain set of stories the culture

By explaining company values through stories the abstract values become tangible. The complex becomes concrete.

of innovation has been maintained. These stories have become the building blocks for the dynamic company culture of 3M.

CASE

For more than 50 years, the company has been acutely aware of the role that story-telling can play in developing the values and culture.

A Playground for Idea Makers

"Pioneering work and storytelling has always been an important part of the 3M company culture: the stories about those pioneers forming the basis for 3M's basic message – innovation. And by reading those stories it becomes easier to understand 3M's eagerness to challenge conventions and encourage new, innovative solutions for both small and large problems and needs."

The above paragraph comes from 3M's website. For more than 50 years, the company has been acutely aware of the role that storytelling can play in developing the values and culture that have enabled 3M to successfully maintain its high rate of innovation.

When 3M was founded in 1902, it produced sandpaper. Today 3M is a highly diversified company doing business in a wide number of fields including electronics, chemicals, construction, healthcare, office supplies and communication. The various divisions of 3M however, all have the same basic passion driving them forward: innovation and finding better solutions in their field. This has made 3M one of the most respected companies in the USA.

The story behind the invention of 3M's classic post-it note, can be found in numerous management books as an example of how a company can further a culture of innovation:

"Our story begins in 1968 when 3M-scientist, Dr. Spencer Silver, set out to develop a new kind of super glue with extraordinary sticking capabilities. The glue was intended for use in 3M's many wallpaper products. But Silver's project failed. At least, that's what they thought at first. In the course of his experiments Silver came upon a glue of a very different nature; one that had unusually low sticking capabilities. He knew that he had found something quite extraordinary, but he had no idea what to use it for. Over the next five years Silver held a number of seminars for his colleagues enthusiastically telling them about this new glue.

Curiously, it turned out that the real breakthrough did not come from the hands of Spencer Silver at all, but from another 3M scientist who had taken part in one of Silver's seminars. The scientist was Arthur Fry. Fry sang in his local church choir and had an ongoing problem in that the bookmarks in his psalm book kept falling out. In a moment of inspiration, he suddenly remembered Spencer's glue and thought about how it would be perfect for bookmarks. He experimented by putting a dab of Spencer's glue on a bookmark and sticking it into his book. Voila, it worked like a dream. The bookmark stayed in place nicely, but he could easily remove it without damaging his psalm book. Thus the idea for 3M's popular post-it notes was born. An idea which now generates annual sales worth approximately US$ 100 millions."

Another chapter in the story is the clever way in which the idea was pitched to management. Employees started using the little yellow notes within the company, displaying its functionality for all to see. Instead of droning on about why the idea was so ingenious, they let the product talk for itself at the same time letting management see for themselves what it was capable of.

In the story archives of 3M, there are innumerable similar stories. Like the story of the female 3M-scientist, Patsy Sherman, who invented a unique protective agent for textiles. Back in 1953, Patsy Sherman noticed a seemingly unimportant incident. An assistant in Sherman's laboratory had spilled a few drops of an experimental chemical on her new trainers. Naturally the assistant was upset, thinking that she wouldn't be able to get the stains off. Nothing worked; soap, alcohol or other solvents. Sherman however, became fascinated with the chemicals incredible resilience and began forming an idea, which at the time seemed ridiculous: to develop a chemical that could repel water and oil from cloth fabrics. By 1956, Scotchgard™ Protector was launched, marking the beginning of a whole new range of highly successful Scotchgard™ products. The brand has been the market leader ever since.

These stories are not only about successes, but also about projects that failed.

A popular saying at 3M is that you have to kiss an awful lot of frogs before you find your prince. They are pragmatists. Failing is par-for-the-course when it comes to innovation and product development. These stories are not only about successes, but also about projects that failed.

Internally, it is authentic stories like these that nurture and nourish a company culture where inventors are heroes providing employees with the conviction that the next blockbuster-product is just around the corner. These stories are also used in the recruiting process, to explain to new employees how things work at 3M. Instead of paper mountains describing each step in the process of getting a green light for a proposed project, all new employees are told stories about legendary product developers who challenged the system and got their projects approved. A classic case of, if you believe in something strongly enough, your dreams will come true.

Outside of company walls, these stories give customers and partners an image of 3M as an extraordinarily visionary company, and a leader in innovation: a glowing example of how a core story works as a catalyst for the company's brand, both internally and externally. 3M's core story is about "innovation at all cost". It fights a daily battle to make our lives easier through new inventions. The adversaries in the story are all the things that

What is the Message of Your Story?

Any story is open to interpretation depending on the person listening. But the way the story is told and the ending of the story are also important. Hence, we need to bear in mind how we want the story to be interpreted before we start telling it. As storytellers, we must be aware of exacting the interpretation that we want the listener to reach.

How do you interpret the following story:
Once, two young and inexperienced product developers of a large company had what they thought to be a good idea. But despite their passion, management remained sceptical. When they presented their idea they were told to drop the project. But the keen young product developers did not give up. They continued tinkering with their idea in their spare time and when it came time to decide what projects the company was going to prioritise for the coming year, they presented their idea again. This time they succeeded in convincing management to go ahead with the project. Today the product is one of the company's topselling items.

What is the moral of the story?
· That management is incompetent?
· That the company's decision-making process is too slow?
· That willpower and belief in one's ideas pay off in the end?

Would your interpretation of the story change if the last three words "top selling items" were replaced with "biggest failures"? The point is, often it takes only a very few changes to alter the possible interpretations of a story. We need to meticulously work with everything from wording to intonation to get our message across as intended.

A Tool for Knowledge Sharing

By exchanging stories we also share knowledge.

Stories communicate values. But they also communicate knowledge. By exchanging stories we also share knowledge. It is said, that stories are easier to remember and recount than naked information. This is basically because, in stories, information is packaged in a meaningful context for us to better understand the depth and the relevance of the information being relayed. Some scientists believe that stories stimulate the use of the logical and creative parts of our brain at the same time. This means that we understand the information factually as well as visually and emotionally.

So, storytelling can also be a good way to share and store knowledge in the organisation. Several knowledge-based companies are making targeted use of storytelling as a knowledge sharing or knowledge management tool. In these companies, knowledge is worth millions. Yet, far too much knowledge is lost due to its not being shared across departments and between employees. In order to preserve this highly valuable knowledge, employee stories are being gathered and systemised making them available to the rest of the organisation.

CASE

IBM has conducted continuous studies as to how and why stories make a difference when it comes to sharing knowledge among employees.

Sharing Knowledge Through Stories at IBM

IBM has both internal and external experience with storytelling. Internally, they have made targeted use of storytelling for a number of specific projects. For example, storytelling is used in relation to change or integration processes like the merging of two departments. Additionally, IBM also uses storytelling when sharing and embedding knowledge in the company.

As part of their work with knowledge management, IBM has also conducted continuous studies as to how and why stories make a difference when it comes to sharing knowledge among employees. One of their basic premises is that stories provide a simple and easily understandable means of communicating a complex problem. The following anecdote has been used many times to illustrate this exact point:

The Slow Elevator

A few years ago, the tenants in a Manhattan office high-rise complained vigorously about the long wait for the elevators. Computer programmers were brought in to change the algorithms, but the complaints got worse. New, faster motors were installed at considerable expense, but the complaints continued and many tenants threatened to move out. In desperation, the owner hired structural engineers to estimate the cost of installing additional elevator shafts. But the cost of installation, along with the reduced amount of rent-able space would have been ruinous. At this point the owner's cousin suggested putting mirrors next to the elevators. They did, and the complaints stopped.

According to IBM, the anecdote describes how we draw hasty conclusions as to the cause of a problem in a given situation. The owner of the skyscraper was quick to identify the speed and effectiveness of the elevators as the problem, instead of looking into how the unpleasantness of the wait could be reduced. This in itself is a complex message, but through the story the point becomes beautifully simple. A story helps us identify the moral and the meaning, and thus it gives us a better basis for making the right decisions.

A story helps us identify the moral and the meaning, and thus it gives us a better basis for making the right decisions..

Based on this philosophy IBM has used storytelling in numerous contexts for sharing complex knowledge between employees. In the USA, IBM has employed a somewhat unusual method for sorting the valuable knowledge gained from finished projects. When IBM initiates and implements large projects in the million-dollar range, the process often spans several years. This makes each individual project unique, and no matter whether it is a success or a failure each project contributes valuable experiences and insight. In order to keep this knowledge from being lost and forgotten, the employees involved are asked to re-tell the process together. The session is videotaped, analysed and made available to relevant personnel in the company. The result is a catalogue of best practice stories that help IBM to constantly improve its business while strengthening the brand from within. The approach is simple: group meetings in theatrical style. So is the technology: a video camera.

Xerox decided to gather "coffee break stories" and structure them in an easily accessible database.

By digging out stories and systemising them, management can prevent important information from being lost or isolated in specific departments. The large copier manufacturer, Xerox, came to the same conclusion some years ago. An internal investigation revealed that rather than looking in manuals or using expensive training courses, the most commonly used method for Xerox repair and service personnel to exchange information on how to deal with various problems in the field, was to swap stories by the coffee machine or water cooler: a revelation that management soon put to good use. Xerox decided to gather these "coffee break stories" and structure them in an easily accessible database named Eureka: a database for "aha" experiences. According to Head Researcher John Seely Brown, Eureka saves Xerox in excess of US$ 100 million annually.

Spearheaded by Knowledge Director, Dave Snowden, IBM's work using storytelling as an internal management tool has increased the focus on how to counter the increasing complexity of modern organisations. When the complexity of an organisation increases along with the conditions for accurate planning, traditional management methods like scenario forecasting often fall short of the objective. IBM has even established an entire centre – The Cynefin Centre – that only works with management and knowledge sharing in complex organisations. The centre's purpose is to develop tools for problem solving in companies where traditional management methods have failed. A large database of stories will be a central part of this toolbox. The centre is going to work as a global network based on the membership of both companies and individuals. ■

Kick Starting Your Company's Storytelling-circulation

There are many applications for storytelling in the internal branding process. Stories can be used to communicate visions and values, to strengthen company culture, to manage the company through change and to share knowledge across the organisation.

No matter what purpose the company may have in using storytelling internally, management needs to be clear about one thing: storytelling is a dynamic and continuous process. First the stories have to be identified and gathered, then they must be sorted and processed and finally they have to be communicated to the organisation in the right way. What follows is a continuous effort to make employees take ownership of these stories in order to keep them embedded in the company. The circulation has to be maintained otherwise the long-term effect will dissipate. Before the process can begin however, the company must define a clear objective for the storytelling project. Criteria must be set as to what the stories have to communicate, which values those stories should support, and what employees should gain from those stories?

In order to establish a storytelling-circulation the company has to go through the following phases:

1) Searching
   First the stories have to be gathered. This can be done via workshops or interviews with selected key personnel.

2) Sorting
   The stories are listed and those with depth and relevance for the objective of the project are selected for further processing.

3) Shaping

The selected stories are processed according to the four elements of storytelling in order to make them "tell-able". Does the individual story have a logical sequence of actions with a conflict? Is there a hero and an adversary? Is the message clearly communicated?

4) Showing

Finally the stories are given a format in which to be communicated to employees. This may be done in the form of small video shorts on the company Intranet, or a story booklet handed out to individual employees. At the same time a strategy should be put in place for introducing the stories to the organisation in such a way that makes them visible and relevant to the right people.

5) Sharing

For management, the task is to ensure that these stories are told continuously and in the relevant contexts so that employees can take ownership of the stories. When employees can see and understand the idea, they will be able to contribute with new stories and collecting company stories becomes an ongoing process: The storytelling circulation has been initiated. Finally, management should consider how the company could establish a forum enabling employees to share their stories.

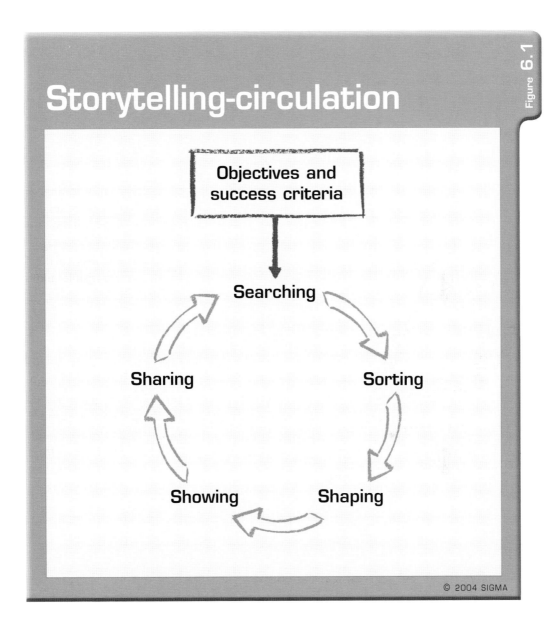

Figure 6.1

Storytelling-circulation

Objectives and success criteria

Searching

Sorting

Sharing

Shaping

Showing

© 2004 SIGMA

Storytelling in Advertising 7

In traditional advertising, storytelling is used as part of the company's corporate branding strategy and as a sales promotional tool to generate recognition and identification. This chapter gives various examples and different angles for using storytelling as the central driving force in advertising.

Within the advertising industry storytelling is a given; an ever-present element in the sense that commercials have always told stories. Likewise, they have always used the four elements of storytelling in their pursuit of achieving consumer awareness and loyalty, be it through television, radio, magazines, bill-boards, or, on the Internet.

That said increased consciousness of the power of storytelling has also left its mark on traditional advertising. Today, we see commercials using the art of storytelling in its purest form, especially as companies experience an increasingly urgent need to differentiate themselves from the competition, while giving their consumers an added-value experience that transcends the actual products. More and more companies are looking to create a story universe surrounding their products and services. In so doing, their story becomes the driving force behind their brand values, separating them from the grey masses.

More and more companies are looking to create a story universe surrounding their products and services.

The Commercial Serial as a Long-term Platform
A phenomenon in advertising, which was developed during the late 1980s and throughout the 1990s, is the concept of running TV-commercials as a serial. Inspired by the style and tone

of feature movies and different television formats including soap operas, dramas and sit-coms, the action spans several individual episodes that uphold the overall story. The rise of the commercial-serial seems to be a manifestation of storytelling in the world of advertising that has taken the genre into a realm as creative and sophisticated as filmmaking. The trademark of the serial, is that that the product and price focus is set aside, in favour of a story that aims to entertain and involve the audience emotionally; in much the same way as we become involved in television series and feature films.

The product and price focus is set aside in favour of a story that aims to entertain and involve the audience emotionally.

The strength of a good story is that it can evolve over time. The characters get the space they need to develop their personalities and we get to know them better. If we can identify with the characters, the chances are we will embrace the story. And as the conflict drives the story forward, we become more deeply involved and the commercial message is transmitted more easily, almost without our realising it. Thus, whether the purpose is to sell a product, increase brand recognition or strengthen the company's image, the advantage of the commercial serial is that it creates a long-term platform for the company to communicate its messages, and establishes a long term relationship with the viewer.

The popular television series, *Moonlighting*, which starred Bruce Willis and Cybil Shepherd paved the way for the first commercial serial in 1987, when Nestlé launched their campaign for NESCAFÉ Gold Blend in England. This would later prove to be one of the most enduring and popular advertising campaigns in British history.

Love Over Gold

Up until 1987, English commercials for NESCAFÉ Gold Blend coffee had focused entirely on the product, emphasising the golden coffee bean as a symbol of their high quality coffee. But

CASE

Nestlé was up against a challenge. Even though NESCAFÉ Gold Blend was doing well and had gained a position in the market as a gourmet coffee, the brand was not accessible to the majority of the buying public. It was really only known among coffee connoisseurs, and the rational product-focussed message was only interesting to this limited audience. Nevertheless, NESCAFÉ Gold Blend was widely recognised: a fact, which Nestlé turned to their advantage. The objective was to keep the brand's position as a gourmet coffee, but to reposition it as a coffee with a broad appeal that was accessible to everybody. The solution was to tell a story that would get the consumer emotionally involved in the brand.

The Nestlé commercial serial, Love Over Gold, *was the closest a commercial had ever come to being a soap opera.*

The change from a rational product focus to an emotional universe resulted in a romantic every day drama with wide public appeal. The Nestlé commercial serial, *Love Over Gold,* was the closest a commercial had ever come to being a soap opera. The commercials introduced two main characters – a man and a woman – who were neighbours in an upper-class apartment complex. From the onset it was clear to everyone that they were made for each other, the script oozed sexual innuendo. But each time you thought the couple were going to get together over a cup of NESCAFÉ Gold Blend, small occurrences kept interrupting them and getting in their way. Each episode ended on an emotional high with an unresolved ending, and as the chemistry and the flirting increased, the audience were likewise, left wanting more. This curiosity soon turned into addiction as audiences followed each episode to find out if the flirtation would ever blossom into an actual romance.

The English public took this small every day drama to heart, especially women. The secret to its success? Emotional involvement. The actual product – instant coffee that tasted like the real thing – was a natural element in the story, but it was love and romance that communicated the message.

The first series was so popular that Nestlé decided to make twelve episodes instead of the original six. They ran for five years. It culminated with a bonanza showing all the original commercials and a fairy-tale ending in which viewers saw the happy couple disappearing into the sunset. More than 30 million viewers tuned in to see our hero finally utter the words "I love you". The next day, the two main characters were on the cover of The Sun. The story of the campaign led to two CDs and a video, and in 1993 a new series was aired, introducing a new couple that repeated the success.

More importantly, since 1987 NESCAFÉ Gold Blend has increased its sales by 60%.

The campaign for NESCAFÉ Gold Blend was clearly structured on the four elements of storytelling, and this example clearly shows how storytelling can make a difference in traditional marketing, provided the story has a solid structure and directly addresses the target audience. Taking its starting point in the values behind NESCAFÉ Gold Blend – "good taste" and "passion" – an entertaining story was told which got viewers' attention. The focus was on the characters and the action while the product took a back seat, though it still managed to play a crucial role in the development of the story. ∎

A French Affair

CASE

This was also the case when French car manufacturer, Renault, launched the new Clio – the successor to their long-established Renault 5 – in the UK, March 1991. Renault wanted to build a long-term communication platform that would continue to enhance consumer awareness and create a strong brand position for the Clio.

Extensive research prior to the campaign showed that the British public strongly aspired to the French way of life, believing it offered a more relaxed, romantic and desirable lifestyle than their own. This was further supported by the fact that 6.8 million Britons said that after the UK, France was next in their preferred places to live, and that 2.2 million Britons visited France in 1990 alone. Another indication was the phenomenal success of *A Year in Provence* by Peter Mayle, which sold over 150,000 copies in the UK and was on the top-seller list for 42 weeks.

Instead of producing a traditional car advertisement focussing only on the product, Renault decided to develop a story universe around the Clio brand.

For Renault, this obsession with French culture was a great opportunity to set the course for a new, creative approach to advertising. Instead of producing a traditional car advertisement focussing only on the product, Renault decided to develop a story universe around the Clio brand. One that was capable of conveying the appeal of French values and lifestyle, thus appealing to peoples' emotions and making the message of the new Clio more relevant to the target group. Renault launched a campaign that told a story about the French and their romances, at the same time introducing the two main characters Nicole, a chic, beautiful young woman, and her father "Papa".

Set in scenic Provence, the first 60-second commercial showed Nicole in a polka dot summer frock, sneaking past her sleeping "Papa" in the garden of their Chateau and driving away in her Renault Clio to meet with her boyfriend. Having faked his sleep "Papa" then goes off on *his* own rendezvous with a lady friend. Upon their return, they greet each other with "Nicole?" and "Papa!" The commercial ends with the strap line, "Renault: a Certain Flair."

The scene was set and the campaign quickly became part of British life. The following year a sequel was released and eventually the series became a saga, airing for more than seven years. It shot Nicole – 21-year-old actress Estelle Skornik – into national stardom. In 1996, a survey found that Nicole was recognised by more Britons than Prime Minister John Major,

to let people discover and interact with the brand in the digital world. BMW set out on an advertising quest that would ultimately blur the zone between films, entertainment and advertising. By merging the best of BMW with the best of Hollywood, they created a truly innovative storytelling universe.

By merging the best of BMW with the best of Hollywood, they created a truly innovative storytelling universe.

The solution was radical – and expensive. BMW teamed up with some of the best directors in the world to create a collection of original short films about a mythical driver and his adventures in his BMW. Costs for filming were covered by BMW and while each film featured one of the company's automobiles, the filmmakers were given complete creative control. With their own unique points-of-view each director would create a short film designed to entertain and exploit the power and brand of BMW. Research had shown that 85% of BMW consumers first went online to scope out the company's portfolio, before purchasing vehicles. Therefore, the concept was not to create a mainstream film release for theatres, but rather bring the power and quality of feature-length movies to a format designed for the Internet. Reaching out to a global audience, the collection of short films was to be viewed on BMWfilms.com in superb streaming video quality.

The campaign entitled *The Hire* was launched in 2001 as a collection of five to seven minute films featuring famous faces, sexy cars and high-speed action. Executive produced by David Fincher (*Seven, Fight Club*) the films were created by prolific directors such as Ang Lee and Guy Ritchie. The constant main character in each short film, the hero, was actor Clive Owen (*The Bourne Identity, Gosford Park* and *Croupier*) who features as the mysterious, unnamed driver-for-hire. Hired for his superb driving skills he encounters unexpected obstacles that put his abilities to the test. In each short he gets involved with famous, mysterious clients seeking different destinations while being hunted by thuggish gangs and fanatical paparazzi. On his quest he is accompanied by a star studded supporting cast including, among others Ray Liotta, Gary Oldman, James Brown and Madonna. Besides creative plot twists, the films of course feature thrilling car chases and nail-biting stunts that display the myriad ability of various BMW models.

BMW's story The Hire *at www.BMWfilms.com.*

Across the States, critics hailed *The Hire* as "groundbreaking". TIME magazine called it the "ultimate in new media, high-end branding". BMWfilms.com was the "advertainment" hit of the year with more than 14 million film viewers registered on the BMWfilms.com site throughout 2001. Throughout May 2002, BMW sales in the US went up by 17.4% compared to the same period the year before. Competitors General Motors and Volkswagen sales meanwhile were suffering.

After the success of these first movies, BMW used the momentum the following year to create a new sequence of films – also as a means to launch BMW's next generation roadster, the BMW Z4. BMW even hired new actors and directors around their hero, Clive Owen to keep the films fresh. The second instalment of *The Hire* added executive producers Tony Scott,

Ridley Scott and Jules Daly, and director John Woo to the dream team.

"*The Hire* is a concept that invites and challenges a director's imagination", said Ridley Scott. "It's great that we are able to partner with BMW on a series which has already had such an effect on pop culture and heavily impacted the world of film and the Internet".

The success of the BMW filmmaking project inspired their backyard rivals at Mercedes to enter into the world of story-telling too, only this time in a slightly different direction. Mercedes also spent vast sums of money on a celebrity cast that included Benecio del Tory and Oscar-nominated director, Michael Mann. This time the plot centred on a professional gambler named Mr. H who worked the big casinos, eventually attracting the attention of government agents.

The success of the BMW filmmaking project inspired their backyard rivals at Mercedes to enter into the world of storytelling too.

The key difference in Mercedes' approach to this world of advertainment, was that their campaign film was presented as a two and a half minute trailer for an upcoming movie *Lucky Star* on ITV, Channel 4 and at select cinemas. All through the trailer Del Toro was shown driving Mercedes' sleek new convertible sports car, the Mercedes logo was never shown and the company's name never appeared. The only connection was the title *Lucky Star* referring to the Mercedes iconic logo, which is among the most recognised brand icons in the world. The trailer finished with a teaser: "*Lucky Star*, coming soon to a theatre near you. See press for details". But there was no *Lucky Star* coming soon to any theatre anywhere. What appeared to be a movie trailer was in fact a commercial for the new Mercedes SL-Class sports car. The link to the Mercedes brand was never obvious to the unknowing audience and the trailer generated plenty of hype before people realised that Mercedes was behind the hoax.

Mercedes collected full data on 14,000 prospective drivers, which ultimately led to the recruitment of 3,000 test drivers.

This approach earned Mercedes the ear of a younger target audience and had some pay-off. The original directors cut of the movie was viewed 50,000 times over a four-week period on the official web-site www.luckystar.com. Mercedes collected full data on 14,000 prospective drivers, which ultimately led to the recruitment of 3,000 test drivers.

Looking at the BMW and Mercedes-Benz campaigns, it seems only a matter of time before one of them produces a full-length feature movie. In that case, however, it would not be the first time. The first company to transform a commercial serial into to an actual feature-length movie was Danish mobile telephone company Sonofon. The story of a naive and loveable hillbilly by the nickname of "Polle" who desperately struggled to figure out how to use his new mobile phone became so popular in Denmark, that the company decided to extend the story and finance a whole movie production. In 2002 *Polle Fiction* hit the big screen, becoming one of the top 3 Danish films to sell the largest number of tickets on the premier night.

Storytelling can take on a variety of forms in the universe of advertising. Largely, it simply comes down to creating a recognisable and relevant universe where the company or its products take on a natural role in the story. But it is the characters and their actions, and the conflicts they try to resolve that drive the story forward. The story however, can only be effective if on some level we can identify with the characters; if we are able to laugh at them or recognise ourselves in the way they behave.

Use Well-known Stories

Many commercials make use of storytelling by referring to, or, borrowing from stories that already exist. By using an already established story, the stage is set for your company to place its product or message in an existing story universe without having to explain everything from scratch. The launch of the

Apple Macintosh computer in 1984 was a strong example of how to use this kind of storytelling in a commercial. The commercial *1984* became a true classic, and was recently awarded the best advertising campaign in the past 50 years by World Federation Advertisers.

Apple and 1984

In 1976, Steve Jobs and Steve Wozniak founded the computer manufacturer Apple, in California. Even back in those days, the company already represented the human side of computer technology, breaking with norms and the way in which information was traditionally controlled within society.

CASE

The Macintosh was far more than just another new product when it was launched in 1984. To Apple, it was a technological revolution that would change the world. This theme formed the basis for Apple's adaptation of the universe created in George Orwell's classic, *1984*, in the advertising for the launch of the new Macintosh. The science fiction novel describes a totalitarian society where The Party controls all information and brainwashes the populace to adhere to the demands of the system. People are under constant supervision and the fear of The Party's mind police is ever present. But beneath the surface, a revolution quietly simmers.

With reference to the book, *1984*, Apple staged itself as the rebel fighting against the establishment. It became a story of how the new Macintosh would provide information technology on the premise of the individual, giving him or her the opportunity to express themselves on their own terms. At the same time, the story painted a poignant picture of what the world might be like without Apple.

With reference to the book, 1984, Apple staged itself as the rebel fighting against the establishment.

The commercial shows a terrifying, prison-like environment populated by a mass of tragic-looking people all wearing the same grey uniforms, all with the same expressionless faces, all marching along like robots. Eventually they congregate in front of a big screen projecting the image of an authoritarian leader who is blazing the words, "Our unification of thought is a more powerful weapon than any fleet, or army on Earth". Simultaneously, the mind police start chasing a colourfully dressed young woman who lunges full speed at the big screen brandishing a large sledgehammer, which splinters it with a terrific crash.   Cut to the message. "On January 24th Apple Computer will introduce Macintosh. And you'll see why 1984 won't be like *1984*". This famous commercial was shot by one of Hollywood's great storytellers, Ridley Scott.

Choosing a story with such overtly political content was both contentious and risqué. Apple placed itself in the role of the hero as the people's saviour, with more than the slightest suggestion that the adversary in the story was Big Blue, IBM. At that time, IBM held a monopoly-like status on the market and was the natural exponent for the cold unification that Apple was rebelling against. Apple's basic message has not changed since. The company's brand has centred on the story of creative diversity and having the courage to think outside the box.

Apple's brand has centred on the story of creative diversity and having the courage to think outside the box.

In a market where the majority of the players compete on price and technology, Apple still places "people" at the centre of everything they do. Technology has to work based on human premises – and not the other way around. Their soft values of individuality and creativity are reflected all the way through to the company logo; an apple of nature, with a bite taken out of it. In spite of fluctuating economical performance Apple has created a strong core story and an extremely loyal customer base all around the globe. ∎

The Meatrix

1984 is of course a classic in advertising history. But tapping into well-known stories as a communication tool does not have to be expensive or high-profile in order to be effective. That is what New York-based activist group, GRACE (The Global Resource Action Center for the Environment) experienced when they launched a campaign to educate the public on the environmental and health risks of factory farming, while promoting support for sustainable food production.

As a non-profit organisation, GRACE had only limited funds for their campaign. So to get their message across they decided on an alternative approach – both creatively and strategically. Their first challenge was to find a way to explain a complex and somewhat unpleasant message to their target audience, especially young urban voters. Their idea, was to exploit the hype around the third movie of the popular science fiction trilogy *The Matrix* featuring Hollywood star Keanu Reeves, by coming up with an online spoof version entitled *The Meatrix*. GRACE simply wrapped up their message in flash animation that ironically played up the plot of the original *Matrix* movie; namely that we are trapped in a world, which is nothing more than an illusion; a computer programmed world that blinds us to the gruesome reality.

Instead of Keanu Reeves, *The Meatrix* stars a young pig by the name of Leo who lives on a pleasant family farm...or so he thinks. In reality, Leo is trapped in the Meatrix – a fantasy world where small, family-run farms still exist. Leo is approached by a cow wearing shades and dressed in a long black trench coat. The cow is the wise and mysterious "Moopheus" who leads the farming resistance. He frees Leo from his delusions and shows him the ugly truth about the business of agriculture: That animals are mass-produced on factory farms, which are cruel to animals and destructive to the environment. *The Meatrix* is

Their idea, was to exploit the hype around the third movie of the popular science fiction trilogy The Matrix.

the lie we tell ourselves about where our food comes from, Moopheus explains to Leo.

GRACE wrapped up their message in flash animation that ironically played up the plot of the original Matrix movie at www.themeatrix.com.

GRACE's animation argues that many people are still trapped in the Meatrix, believing that farmed animals roam freely on green hills and are gently "put to sleep" before being killed. The reality is, that in many of today's factory farms animals raised for food lead miserable lives.

The pig Leo, eventually joins the resistance to stop factory-farming and free others from the horrors of *The Meatrix*. GRACE asks their audience to do the same by offering a free "Eat Well Guide" at the end of the animation: a national online guide to sustainable-raised meat.

GRACE made a smart strategic move by launching the Internet animation on the same day as the national release of the third *Matrix* movie, cleverly riding the wave of the publicity of the real movie, and thus maximising attention around their own campaign. The low budget production became an explosive online hit. Barely a week after its launch, *The Meatrix* had been

When Storytelling Becomes Dialogue 8

The role of companies as storytellers has radically changed. Technological development and new digital possibilities are forcing them to pay attention to what their customers are telling them, whether they like what they hear or not. In the following chapter we take a closer look at how digital media provides new opportunities for your company and customers to exchange stories.

Poul Petersen was an ordinary Dane, with an ordinary insurance policy, from an ordinary insurance company; Almindelig Brand Insurance. But he felt that he had been unfairly treated when they denied his claim of 27,000 Euros compensation, for the serious damages caused to his house by a storm. Their handling of the case in his opinion had been extremely poor. He tried in vain to make Almindelig Brand listen to his point of view, but his attempts fell on deaf ears. Then Poul became so bitter that he decided to share his frustrations with the rest of the world. Poul built a simple website titled *Screwed by the Insurance Company*, where he told his story. It marked the beginning of a nightmare for Almindelig Brand. The story was good, it had great conflict and the rumour of the website spread like wildfire. By the time the site had reached 25,000 visitors, Poul celebrated its success by hosting an event to which he also invited the CEO of Almindelig Brand (who needless to say, didn't show up.) The party caught the attention of the media and the story ended up in the national news, while Almindelig Brand watched in stunned amazement. The site had reached 80,000 visitors before Poul Petersen finally got his money.

How many Poul Petersens do you have among your customers? It only takes one Poul Petersen before the avalanche gets rolling.

Companies are Losing Power

Companies are losing control over the information exchange and opinion forming that creates their brands. The former, one-way communication channel from company to market is long gone. And, with the advent of the Internet, there has been a permanent shift in the balance of power between company and consumer. Companies can tell their stories from now until the end of the world, but if their stories are out of tune with the stories of their customers, they will backfire sooner or later.

Companies are losing control of the information exchange and the opinion forming that creates their brands.

Through the Internet, consumers are brought together in communities where they can share their opinions. Consumers and interest groups now have the power to mobilise far greater numbers and strength, and get their message out more quickly and clearly than ever before. This means that brands can be created and destroyed in the blink of an eye. Today, anybody with access to the Internet can take on the role of a storyteller with a global audience. It has created a whole new dimension for storytelling.

For companies it is no longer just a question of telling, but a question of listening. Instead of retreating, your company should take advantage of the opportunities this shift offers, by listening to the stories your customers have to tell you.

Involve Your Customers in Your Storytelling

Through our own personal stories we approach each other as humans, build trust and create relationships. The same is true of the relationships created between customer and company. These form the foundation of a strong brand. As improved digital developments create new frameworks for exchanging those stories, they also open up new opportunities for strengthening the company's brand.

The link between branding and storytelling is increasingly pronounced in the digital age.

The link between branding and storytelling is increasingly pronounced in the digital age. The massive exchange of opinions about companies and their products taking place on the Internet is, in itself, a free flowing exchange of stories. They cannot be controlled. But companies can try and catch those stories to get a better picture and understanding of what is being said and why.

Customer stories are a regular oil well, while the Internet offers the perfect drill-bit for accessing them. Several companies have tried to establish a dialogue on the Internet – a sort of organised story or "brand community" if you will. By gathering individual customer stories that can be used strategically in other contexts, your customers get to actively contribute to the making of the company brand. Involving your customers in this way adds serious credibility and substance to your business. Let us look at a few examples of companies that have used the Internet to gather stories.

CASE

The People's Car

Almost half the US population has grown up with a Ford in the family. In the USA, Ford is not just another car. It is a piece of Americana, built on pride and emotional attachment. For a time, visitors to Ford's website were encouraged to contribute their personal Ford-stories – specifically about Ford's four-wheel-drive, off-road truck. One of those stories came from James Flaugher from North Carolina:

"My father and I were going to a job in Northeast Texas and were pulling a gooseneck that was loaded with our sandblasting rig. The two trailers weighed about 17,000 lbs. together. We were following one of the ranchers and came upon a hill about a half a mile long. It was powder-dry red clay, and on top of that, it was very steep. Dad looked over and said, "here we go" and put his foot to the floor. We made it about three quarters of the way up and buried the duals on both sides. The rancher tried to pull us out, but since he only had a two-wheel drive also, he just dug in the powder and nothing happened. We didn't move an inch. Just then we saw an oil field pumper and he was driving a Ford F-350 4x4 off-road. He came up the hill and offered to try to pull us to the top. He tied us on, and just as my dad started to let out the clutch, the pumper gave it that Powerstroke pull and pulled that entire show up the hill without any help from our truck at all. My father looked at me and said, 'my next truck is going to be a 4x4 off-road'. This all happened in 1992, and in 1994 he bought a Powerstroke 4x4 off-road and loves it. We own 14 Fords of all different makes and models in all, including tractors and 18 wheelers."

For a time, visitors to Ford's website, were encouraged to contribute their personal Ford-stories.

As American as this story is, it speaks volumes of the added value Ford gives to their customers. We sense the true affection that the customers feel for the Ford brand. The following story comes from Brian, in Michigan:

"My friend used to tease me about my little Ford 4x4. But the teasing stopped when I pulled his large Dodge Ram 4x4 out of the mud, twice. The same mud that sucked him in was passed over by my little truck like it wasn't there. It's hard to make fun of someone when you're sitting in a truck stuck in the middle of a mud hole."

When collecting stories for your company, it is important to keep in mind what those stories are going to contribute and how they can be used to specifically strengthen the company's brand and support the core story? Ford did not have a particular strategic aim with collecting these stories. They lie hidden far down the order on the corporate website. But in order for the

When collecting stories for your company, it is important to keep in mind what those stories are going to contribute.

stories to have an effect they need to be visible in the right context. Ford dealers could benefit greatly from a small arsenal of stories such as this to use in their daily sales work. ■

Topdanmark's Lucky Heroes

Topdanmark is one of Denmark's leading insurance and pension companies. They market themselves under the pay-off, "Sometimes you get lucky, and sometimes it's good to have Topdanmark". In 2002 the company launched their message with a TV campaign. At the same time people were encouraged to visit the company's website and share a good-luck story from their own lives. Visitors to the site could then vote for the best story and take part in a draw with prize money worth DKK 50,000 (app. 6700 Euros). One of the nominees was a story titled *The Rusty Hand Grenade*:

"When I was 10 years old my friend and I were riding our BMX-bikes in the woods when something in the gravel caught my eye. I stopped and jumped off my bike to take a closer look. It was a hand grenade! I picked it up and showed it to my friend; 'Look, a hand grenade. Cool! I'll bring it to school tomorrow'. My friend told me to get rid of it, but I argued that since the split was missing it would have gone off a long time ago, if ever. On the way home my friend wouldn't ride next to me. He said,' If you are going to bring that grenade with you, then you ride 100 meters behind me'. So I did. We got to my friend's house and went to the kitchen where I placed the grenade in the kitchen sink. His mom came out and I asked if I could borrow a brush. She asked what for, and I told her that I would like to wash the rust from the grenade. When she saw the grenade she went mad and told me to wash it at my own house. I rode home, and on the front lawn my dad was raking the grass. I showed him the grenade, 'Look dad a hand grenade' My dad dropped the rake and yelled at me to put the grenade down at once. I put the grenade in a flowerbox, and my dad told me to get out of there. He ran in the house and ushered the family out the back door, and then he called the police. The police sent the military to come pick up the grenade, and it wasn't until later that I learned how lucky I had actually been. The hand grenade could have gone off at any moment. The split was gone and all that kept the grenade form going off was the rust. The military took the grenade and blew it up."

How lucky can a guy get? The competition gave Topdanmark a lot of stories, and around 21,000 people, out of Denmark's population of 5 million, voted. If you were visiting the site to vote and were not already a Topdanmark customer you automatically received an offer for new insurance. In this way the campaign had a sales target too. But Topdanmark also secured the rights to the stories sent in, so that they could use the stories in other contexts in the future.

As in many other fields of business, most insurance companies offer very similar products. They all look alike and therefore have a difficult time explaining why it is that we should buy their insurance policy as opposed to somebody else's. The solution? You create an "experienced" difference. Topdanmark waved a sizeable prize of DKK 50,000 under the noses of the people who helped them gather their stories about luck, but they also appealed to people's emotions: Tell us about a time when you got extremely lucky. All of us have experienced situations like that. Today we can laugh about them, but when it happened, it was perhaps too scary or shocking to think about. By appealing to those feelings Topdanmark moved the main focus away from their product and created a fresh approach to establishing dialogue with potential customers.

Insurance companies offer very similar products. Therefore they have a difficult time explaining why it is that we should buy their insurance policy as opposed to somebody else's.

But does this use of storytelling strengthen the Topdanmark brand? Certainly, they support Topdanmark's pay-off. But none of the stories submitted had any specific relation to Topdanmark. None talked about why Topdanmark itself makes a difference. Basically they were generic stories that could easily have been told by any other insurance company.

Herein lies an ever-present challenge when companies use storytelling. A story only gains real substance when it clearly shows why your company makes a difference. Otherwise your competitors can simply copy the story. Topdanmark's goal was to take ownership of the concept by having the company brand linked to the idea of being "lucky" or "unlucky". In other words when you think of being "lucky" you should think of Topdanmark. The question is, does this create a long-term foundation for a strong brand? The "lucky" concept is not really rooted in an attitude or a deep felt value anchored in the Topdanmark Company, and it may well prove difficult for Topdanmark to use the concept in the long-term branding process.

The American coffee shop, Starbucks Coffee managed to create a more explicit and natural link to their corporate brand when they launched a similar storytelling initiative in an attempt to establish a dialogue with their consumers. ■

CASE

A Match Made Over Coffee

Over the years employees at Starbucks had heard story after story of customer romances getting started in Starbucks coffee houses. There were in fact stories about people who had met their future wives and husbands at Starbucks – and a couple of times, people had even gotten married at Starbucks. People seemed to genuinely open-up in the casual, laid-back ambience of Starbucks coffee-houses.

So the company decided to try to capture some of these stories and celebrate them with customers and media as part of a Valentine's Day push. The company believed that sharing these human stories would reinforce the idea that Starbucks is a great destination for a date or a chance meeting.

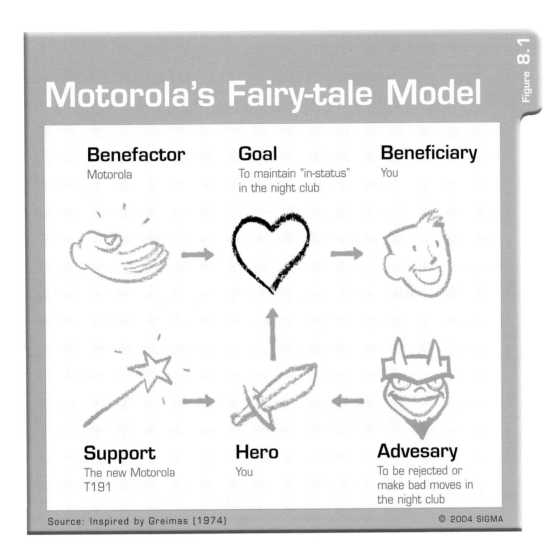

Motorola's Fairy-tale Model

Figure 8.1

Benefactor
Motorola

Goal
To maintain "in-status"
in the night club

Beneficiary
You

Support
The new Motorola
T191

Hero
You

Advesary
To be rejected or
make bad moves in
the night club

Source: Inspired by Greimas (1974)   © 2004 SIGMA

The story was driven forward by the challenges the user had to overcome in order to gain points. He or she had to prove whether they were *in* or not, based on whether they could figure out how to win points in the night-club of the stars using the Motorola mobile phone as a means to achieving that goal. The campaign used a number of words and symbols already used by the target audience. At the same time, the story used the mobile phone as a status symbol and a "must-have" when it comes to

Motorola brand has a visible position in the story and is explicitly connected to the "in" status.

successful social interaction with friends. The Motorola brand had a visible position in the story and is explicitly connected to the "in" status, and the ability to manoeuvre socially in cool circles such as a nightclub.

Besides banner advertising, the game of PartyMoto was spread virally as users recommended the game to their friends. In order to participate, users had to register on the web-site creating an even bigger potential customer database for the company to build on. ∎

Digital Storytelling – Something for Everyone

At the start of the 1990s when the Internet was still making its first tentative steps, a small movement sprung up in the USA around the phenomenon of digital storytelling.

The examples we have looked at so far show how companies today have begun using the vast array of digital possibilities as a means for creating dialogue with their target audience and getting them involved in a story. But the fusion between storytelling and the digital media is far from new. At the start of the 1990s, when the Internet was still making its first tentative steps, a small movement sprung up in the USA around the phenomenon of digital storytelling.

At first, digital storytelling sounded like one of those fancy management buzz-words, but it was actually a grassroots phenomenon. It began among a group of artists and creatives who were driven by the idea of fusing new digital tools with the need for human beings to tell and share their stories. It was also a rebellion against the established media's monopoly on storytelling.

Digital storytelling is a two-part process: 1) digital production and 2) digital distribution. The digital revolution means that ordinary people can begin producing their own little stories using a computer. By digitally mixing pictures, animation, video, text, sound and music we are given a number of tools to enhance the message in our story. But digital storytelling is also about using the Internet as a means of distribution. By launching our stories in the "global movie theatre" we can share our experiences with each other.

The Godfather of digital storytelling was the American, Dana Atchley (1941-2000), who in 1993 took the title of *Digital Storyteller*. Atchley used his own life story as a starting point. He amassed a huge amount of material – old family photos, letters, drawings, music, interviews and old movies and edited the material together on his Apple-computer, eventually ending up with a series of small stories documenting the important events in his life. These experiments became the foundation of an interactive live performance he named *NextExit*.

The Godfather of digital storytelling was the American, Dana Atchley.

With *NextExit*, Dana Atchley attained guru-status among the growing number of digital storytellers in the USA. Creative personalities adopted the phenomenon in order to express their art and tell their stories. In 1995 in an attempt to further spread the idea, Dana Acthley set up the first annual *Digital Storytelling Festival*. Here you could see digital stories in the making, as participants learned how to use the digital tools for storytelling. Later Atchley expanded his work as a digital storyteller and started counselling companies in the art of digital storytelling including Apple, Coca-Cola and Pinnacle Systems.

Tearing Down the Walls 10

"...and they all lived happily ever after."

We are all familiar with the ending of most classical fairy-tales. The conflict has been resolved, the moral has been delivered and the prince has won his princess and half the kingdom. This book has no such happy ending. But it does have an open ending that offers further food for thought.

During the course of this book we have come full circle. We have looked at the four elements that constitute a good story. We have seen how storytelling can be used as a communication tool to strengthen the company's brand in various contexts, both internally and externally. And ultimately, we have established that all of a company's stories must point in the same direction in order to support the company's one core story. This is the precondition for creating a consistent brand that can penetrate a rapacious and noisy market.

Storytelling and branding are inextricably linked with another fundamental issue of strategic communication: holistic thinking

Looking at the bigger picture, it becomes clear that storytelling and branding are inextricably linked with another fundamental issue of strategic communication: holistic thinking. In the end, storytelling is a powerful and creative branding tool, yes, but it is no miracle cure.

Stop Thinking in the Box!

Your customers get information about your company from all manners of different sources: the Internet, newspapers, television commercials, through customer services at the store, over the telephone, or, through friends and colleagues. At the same time, they are also in direct contact with your company's products. If all of these contact points do not provide a consistent experience for your customer, your brand loses power and credibility. Your core story is not being consolidated.

To this end, your core story must be anchored throughout the entire organisation and integrated across different departments and sections. This is the only way that the company can create and project a consistent "face" outwardly. But this is no easy task; there are walls, which must come down.

Dividing walls provide an image of the box thinking that separate company departments in more than just the physical sense: marketing are responsible for advertising; sales are responsible for selling and customer care; production are responsible for manufacturing products; human resources are responsible for personnel development and here in communications, we are responsible for public relations. It is true we all have roles to fulfil, but first and foremost the various departments are part of the same brand, and are all equally responsible for its creation and development. To be truly holistic and to put forward a pure, strong message, all departments must share the same values and communicate the same core story, no matter the context.

Dividing walls provide an image of the box thinking that separate company departments in more than just the physical sense.

Every single employee within his, or, her field must act as an individual ambassador for the company brand. If they do not, the brand will disintegrate from within. Your customers don't care what you call it; PR, marketing, advertising, in-store or customer service, the fact is, whenever they come into contact with your company, the impression you make is stored as a mental image in their minds.

Every single employee must act as an individual ambassador for the company brand. If they do not, the brand will disintegrate from within.

Before management considers using storytelling, their first challenge is to knock down those walls.

Often, this proposition catches management off guard; "But this will require a completely new organisational structure," is the common cry. Well, yes, or at least a new perspective on how things are done. Individual departments can easily remain

When each department creates its own-segmented reality, the dilution of your brand is inevitable.

in place, but their dividing walls – the psychological more so than the physical – have to come down. When each department creates its own-segmented reality, the dilution of your brand is inevitable. There can only be one reality and it is rooted in the company brand. Employees across all different departments have to "live" the same core story. In short, the core brand values have to be anchored tightly within the entire organisation. This is the task facing management and in order for it to be successful, it requires a tightly controlled, top-down approach to communication.

If your organisation cannot project one consistent core story, then how are you going to create a strong brand externally?

If your organisation cannot project one consistent core story, then how are you going to create a strong brand externally? A manager's typical reply would be something along the lines of; "That's what we use advertising for." But in today's consumer savvy climate that is a limited solution. If your employees cannot live up to the promise made to your consumers by the marketing department, it is only a matter of time before your message starts to lose credibility. It is not until the core story has been completely integrated into your organisation – from the inside out – that your company is ready for the holistic approach to external communication that safeguards your company's values.

Let us have a look at an example of what happens when walls separate a company's communication channels.

Candy for Breakfast

For the past 100 years, Kellogg's have been telling the same story about getting the best start to our day by eating a nutritious breakfast. Huge sums of money have been spent on maintaining that story. We see it in commercials, on print advertisements and through in-store promotions in supermarkets.

But in the early 1990s, news broke in Denmark about the disturbingly high sugar and salt content of breakfast cereals.

A sinister scene depicting children eating bowls of candy with spoons accompanied the story. A scare scenario followed, drawing attention to the unhealthy junk that kids were consuming every day for breakfast. In the background, the observant viewer could see a cereal box that looked a lot like one of Kellogg's. The reaction from consumers was immediate and furious, and the entire breakfast cereal category was hit hard. As the market leader, Kellogg's registered a noticeable drop in sales the very next day, with Kellogg's Frosties hit especially hard.

What was not shown, was the fact that Kellogg's invest huge sums of money into nutritional research, just as they do today, in order to safeguard the highest standards. Their mistake was that they had not told their consumers about it. In order to turn around this unfortunate development, Kellogg's initiated a proactive dialogue with nutritional experts about conducting an independent test of the available breakfast cereals. It was a safe gamble. Kellogg's knew that their products were of the highest standard. And the results of the test helped Kellogg's restoring consumer confidence.

Creating a strong core story is not just about having a strong marketing concept. Kellogg's advertising and marketing said one thing. The news segment said another. Their consumers, fearing they had been duped, reacted at once with scepticism and outrage.

From this it is easy to see why a company's core story has to be incorporated into every possible situation, especially where the company is in touch with the external environment. And the core story has to be translated in such a way that it is relevant to all of the company's stakeholders. To Kellogg's, advertising equalled branding. But working within this box mentality tricked the company. Kellogg's had overlooked the fact that the brand also had to be consolidated in other contexts if they were

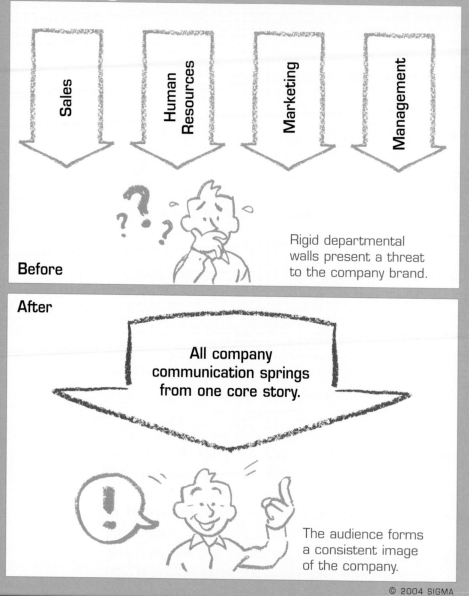

Figure 10.1

Tearing Down the Walls

Sales

Human Resources

Marketing

Management

Before

Rigid departmental walls present a threat to the company brand.

After

All company communication springs from one core story.

The audience forms a consistent image of the company.

© 2004 SIGMA

to ensure a consistent and credible message. Equally, if Kellogg's management team had made sure that the company's nutritionists and marketing department had co-ordinated their efforts and told the same story to their target audience, then Kellogg's could easily have avoided this situation in the first place: instead, internal "box thinking" spilled over into external communication.

This example illustrates why such rigid departmental walls present a threat to the company brand. In Kellogg's world, marketing and dialogue with external nutritionists were two separate issues. In reality though, these are just two communication channels that in the end reach the same audience – the consumer.

Rigid departmental walls present a threat to the company brand.

Once those dividing walls have been destroyed however, you can begin integrating the company's core story into the daily working lives of all your employees. Because, until your departments are streamlined, how can you ensure one consistent message flowing out into the public arena?

Once the dividing walls have been destroyed you can ensure one consistent message flowing out into the public arena.

Are You Getting Your Message Across?

Once your company's core story has been securely anchored within your organisation, it is time to face the second challenge: How to communicate the core story externally?

In his book Permission Marketing, Seth Godin, one of the gurus of Internet Marketing writes that in the course of one year we are exposed to one million commercial messages – that is 3,000 messages every day! 3,000! Just for fun of it, try to think of three commercial messages that you have been exposed to within the last 24 hours? It could be a television commercial, a print advertisement, or a pop-up banner on the Internet. It is not that easy is it? And you are an expert in the field, or at least have some deeper interest in branding and communication otherwise it is unlikely you would have made it all the way to this chapter. How many messages do you think get stored in the memory of an average consumer, considering they probably could not care less about advertising and sales talk? One or two? Three, if we are optimistic? Three out of several thousand! If this is even halfway true, then there must be a lot of companies out there who are wasting an awful lot of money on ineffective marketing.

There must be a lot of companies who are wasting an awful lot of money on ineffective marketing.

Only the companies that really have something to say, and who consistently communicate their message through one core story have a chance of being remembered. But this is not enough. In order to penetrate the noise and be heard and remembered, you need to communicate intelligently. You need to ensure that media support the story's core message making it relevant and interesting for the company's target audience. And once again, this is dependent on a holistic approach.

Many companies have the misconception that traditional advertising is the only thing that drives branding.

Many companies have the misconception that traditional advertising is the only thing that drives branding. Advertising is important, no doubt, but it is far from being the only driver for branding. A company's external communication can be divided into two main categories: commercial and non-commercial messages. Commercial messages are usually sales oriented and include television commercials and other advertising with the company as the messenger. The company directly controls the content of these messages, which has the advantage of communicating exactly what you want, but at the same time reduces your credibility.

Non-commercial messages do not usually have the company as the direct messenger. Typically they are presented in the form of television news stories, or in the printed press. But experts, opinion leaders or consumer groups, can also deliver them. These messages give extra credibility to your brand by the very

Figure 10.2

Commercial vs. non-commercial messages

Messages	Direct messenger	Media	Credibility
Commercial	The company	TV-commercials and ads	Low
Non-commercial	Journalists, consumers, experts or opinion leaders	Articles, expert panels and TV-news segments	High

© 2004 SIGMA

fact that it is a third party, and not your company who is communicating them. Your company cannot buy this kind of statement. You need to have proven yourself worthy in order for independent experts to speak in your favour.

To achieve reach and credibility in its communication, your company needs to employ a combination of commercial and non-commercial messages. And for most companies, their commercial messages clearly outweigh the non-commercial ones.

The Body Shop is a unique example of a company that has managed to manifest its core story mainly through non-commercial messages. In the beginning, the company spent virtually nothing on traditional advertising, living off publicity from media, consumer groups and grassroots movements. This was the primary reason for the high level of respect and credibility that The Body Shop earned in its early years. Within the company, the chains surrounding individual departments had been smashed, but the strategy only worked because the

In the beginning, The Body Shop spent virtually nothing on traditional advertising, living off publicity from media, consumer groups and grassroots movements.

founder of The Body Shop, Anita Roddick, had a strong message that pervaded the entire company. That message was backed by action. The story had substance, and employees lived the brand every day they went to work. Interestingly, since Anita Roddick stepped down as Managing Director in 1998, The Body Shop has experienced some difficulties in maintaining the strength and credibility of its core story.

CASE

oticon

Oticon Conquers the World

The highly regarded manufacturer of hearing aids, Oticon, also tore down its walls in 1997 when the company launched the world's first completely digital hearing aid, DigiFocus. A solid combination of commercial and non-commercial messages paved the way for the worldwide success of the product launch. In Scandinavian business circles, Oticon was already known as the "spaghetti-organisation". This was the name given to the hyper-flexible management style of Lars Kolind, the CEO of Oticon at the time, whose intention was to promote innovation, drive and creativity. But only a very few in the rest of the world, knew who Oticon were. Several industry competitors were hot on their tails in the development of similar digital hearing aids. It was all about getting there first. Oticon was under pressure.

Wrapping their message in the story of The Computer in the Ear, *Oticon created a simple yet powerful image of the digital hearing aid.*

Step one was to develop one unified story as the platform for their campaign. Wrapping their message in the story of *The Computer in the Ear*, Oticon created a simple yet powerful image of the digital hearing aid. A crucial factor in the words and pictures package that is so sought after by media.

Then, Oticon set about developing the foundation of their story in order to maximise credibility. They entered into a proactive dialogue with those professional groups who were expected to be the most critical; their argument being, that if you can convince your worst critics to give you the thumbs up, then you have a bullet proof foundation. In addition to testing the product with consumers – the hearing impaired – Oticon also contacted a number of neurologists, audiologists, brain scientists, IT experts and chip specialists who gave their candid opinion of the product. Their enthusiasm was unprecedented. Experts from a wide variety of backgrounds all jumped to extol the possibilities of the new product.

With this scientific seal of approval and consumer tests as backup, Oticon began to roll out the story six months ahead of the actual launch of the product. Select journalists and media were introduced to the product and the background material. The result was comprehensive global media coverage, which was integrated with commercial messages through TV-commercials, events, direct mails and Internet activities. Through tight management of the communication process, the same unified story of *The Computer in the Ear* was consistently communicated through all channels creating massive interest among trade and end-users, long before the product was even available in stores.

Through tight management of the communication process, the same unified story of The Computer in the Ear *was consistently communicated through all channels.*

DigiFocus became a strong ambassador for the Oticon brand. Oticon was no longer seen as a manufacturing company, but as a pioneer in digital technology. Meanwhile, the company stock rate rose from index 395 to 1,100 in less than a year.

Oticon's stock rate rose from index 395 to 1,100 in less than a year.

An Intelligent Strategy

Oticon's success was no coincidence. The company had meticulously planned an intelligent strategy as to how the story could reach the largest possible audience with the greatest possible impact. First off, Oticon carefully followed the logic of the media. Secondly, the company practised the all important ground rules for communicating one unified message across all media channels, thus ensuring that the audience heard the same story no matter where they went for information.

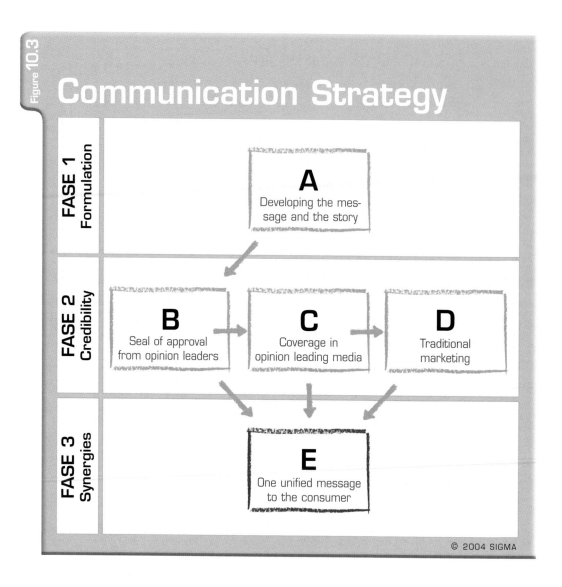

Figure 10.3

Communication Strategy

FASE 1 Formulation

A
Developing the mes-
sage and the story

FASE 2 Credibility

B
Seal of approval
from opinion leaders

C
Coverage in
opinion leading media

D
Traditional
marketing

FASE 3 Synergies

E
One unified message
to the consumer

© 2004 SIGMA

Oticon is far from being the only company to achieve success using this method. Even though the strategy is difficult to control in practice, the basic structure can be roughly illustrated in figure 10.3.

A. Developing the message and the story

The precondition for communicating in the first place is that we have something to say. In order to make our communication efforts relevant to our target audience, any communication strategy must start by developing the story and the central message. Oticon had a groundbreaking product. But the challenge was to develop a good story that concisely explained what made the product so special. The result was the story of *The Computer in the Ear*. It was really about developing the core story for the product brand DigiFocus.

B. Getting a seal of approval from opinion leaders

When both story and message have been developed, the company has to make sure that the story is watertight. The best way to do this is to test your story on your toughest critics. Effectively, that means throwing your message to the lions and seeing what is left once they have gobbled it up. Remember that besides your customers, your toughest critics are usually professional experts and opinion leaders in the field.

Throw your message to the lions and see what is left once they have gobbled it up.

In order to identify the right opinion leaders you need to think backwards. Find out who media go to when they are looking for information about the subject at hand. Who do the media listen to?

Your company should also test the message on opinion leaders from other worlds that have associated relevance within the story. Oticon contacted a wide spectrum of opinion leaders all the way from neurologists and brain scientists, to IT experts and chip specialists. The latter, came from a completely different world than that at Oticon, but they were still highly relevant due to their insight into the latest computer technology. This helped put the story into perspective and show the depth and possibilities of the product; something the audiologists could not have done on their own.

Your company should also test the message on opinion leaders from other worlds that have associated relevance within the story.

The final objective for the company is to ally itself with opinion leaders around the common cause, and communicate the message through and with them. If the story of the company has real substance, then opinion leaders should enjoy the benefits of seeing their own causes linked to the story. Opinion leaders also need to promote themselves on a continuous basis if they are to remain relevant. As a rule of thumb, the company should be able to get a minimum of three independent opinion leaders to give their seal of approval. Three opinion leaders provide sufficient critical mass to eliminate any suspicions of chance.

This is the ultimate test. If the chosen opinion leaders had rejected the Oticon story, there would have been no basis for the strategy as it was carried out. Their opinion determined whether or not the company had to go back and rethink the message. Alternatively, the company can choose to take the conventional way out and try to penetrate the noise of their competitors with traditional marketing tools. But it is costly to yell that loud, and not nearly as credible.

C. Coverage in opinion leading media

An opinion leader's seal of approval provides good leverage for selling the story to the media.

An opinion leader's seal of approval, among other things, provides good leverage for selling the story to the media. If the company has not done its homework the media will soon find holes in the story, but with the support of opinion leaders this risk is dramatically reduced.

The company can also benefit from selling the story to a select few, relevant media that set the agenda within the field of the company. This was a strategy that Oticon used with great success. Once the opinion leading media have picked up the story, the wider media also begin to take an interest in the story. Ultimately, media feed on good stories, and they are constantly seeking inspiration for relevant content for their publications. They also look over each other's shoulders, and use more prolific media as their guide.

D. Traditional marketing

Once you have secured your seal of approval, and your chosen media have picked up on the story, it is time to start employing more traditional forms of marketing. These include in-store activities, commercials and other forms of advertising. On the strength of your non-commercial activities, your commercial messages will appear more credible by creating synergies across media, and directing the same unified message towards the end user (step E in figure 10.3). The timing of the strategy is vital. If traditional marketing is rolled out first, the benefits to be gained from the voices of opinion leaders and media will disappear.

Once you have secured your seal of approval, and your chosen media have picked up on the story, it is time to start employing more traditional forms of marketing.

Most companies overlook this effect. They run on autopilot and roll out the traditional marketing apparatus. They go directly from step A to step D; at best they try to incorporate step C during the process. But often this is a parallel activity that takes place in the shadow of the traditional marketing effort. The true punch is only achieved when even their worst critics can see the potential in the story. This requires serious substance and a near perfect story.

Most companies run on autopilot and roll out the traditional marketing apparatus.

By now you are probably thinking; "It's all well and good to have a nice, simple strategy, but it probably cost Oticon a fortune to launch a global campaign like that". Actually, the answer is "No", especially given the effect. TV-coverage alone was achieved on more than 1,650 stations worldwide. The publicity caused the company's stock value to more than double. If your story is good enough, you can achieve amazing results with creative storytelling techniques and an intelligent strategy, even when your budgets are limited. The launch of the American cult thriller *The Blair Witch Project* is an excellent example of just what you can do, even on the most limited resources.

CASE

Bringing a Legend to Life

The combined investment for the film *The Blair Witch Project* was a meagre 34,000 Euros. But thanks to a clever campaign that ignited the mystery surrounding the movie, *The Blair Witch Project* ended up grossing more than 135 million Euros world-wide. Rumours of a horrifying "true" story were built up by systematically leaking information here and there, and building hype by word-of-mouth one year in advance of the movie premiere.

The rumour was spread that two young movie directors had found eight rolls of film in the woods surrounding the small town of Blair, in Maryland, USA. The tapes shed light on the disturbing fate of three college students, who had gone on an expedition into the woods in order to make a documentary about the mythical Blair Witch that had terrified the local community for centuries. The college students disappeared mysteriously, but thanks to the discovery of eight rolls of film, the truth about what had actually happened to them was finally out and had been made into a movie: a documentary thriller based on a true story. The campaign duped cinema-goers the world over.

In reality, the story was an ingeniously clever scam. The myth of the Blair Witch and the missing college students was the directors' idea.

In reality, the story was an ingeniously clever scam. The myth of the Blair Witch and the missing college students was the directors' idea. But through a carefully planned strategy that moved into an ethical grey area, they managed to distort the relationship between reality and fiction to such a degree that it could well have happened. First the fictive story was told in a limited forum. At selected colleges and trendy hangouts for young people in and around the town of Blair, posters of the missing college students appeared. The posters had pictures of the three under the headline "MISSING". At the same time the directors managed to have a documentary aired on the science fiction channel "SciFi channel", where the story was depicted as an actual event.

On www.blairwitch.com the world could see statements from the people of Blair, photos and newscasts of the event. What nobody knew was that they were watching actors playing the role of police, newscasters and relatives. On the website, there also appeared a historical timeline of all the mysterious events that had occurred in the woods surrounding Blair from the sixteenth century to the present day. They included stories of abducted children, witches, murders, ghosts, legends, strange symbols and insane hermits. The hype was at full throttle and more than 200,000 visitors had logged on to www.blairwitch.com before the movie even got to cinemas.

The hype was at full throttle and more than 200,000 visitors had logged on to www.blairwitch.com before the movie even got to cinemas.

The massive interest also caught the eye of the media. Journalists across the world were quite literally goaded into solving the mystery surrounding the Blair Witch. Like everybody else they were fascinated. Aided by front covers on Time Magazine and Newsweek the myth spread to a worldwide audience. On December 2nd 1999 the Danish paper Politiken wrote, "The truth is, that no matter how you twist and turn *The Blair Witch Project*, it remains a good story, and when it comes to good stories the media has no self control. No matter whether you look at the manipulation, or the 135 million Euros – or whether you actually like the movie – *The Blair Witch Project* is a damn good story, and faced with such, the media are powerless. You think that you are writing critical journalism, but actually you end up in the big black pot, because every line you write, adds to the myth and the blockbuster success. It is the realisation of these interconnected relations and the systematic exploitation of them that remains the greatest trick of the people behind *The Blair Witch Project*."

If the Blair Witch people had launched a traditional campaign via television commercials, print advertisements and billboards, the story would never have gone so far. It would not have had the same credibility and punch. In what amounts to arguably one of the most creative, if deceptive, marketing campaigns in history, *The Blair Witch Project* is an extreme example, but it serves to underline why the way in which we tell our stories, is decisive in the way we perceive it.

The strategy for *The Blair Witch Project* was exemplary. First the story was found. Then the strategy was planned. And finally the story was told in a systematic manner across media that could directly engage the target audience. ■

You Decide the Ending

"Where did Nora go?" The question eats away at all who have read Henrik Ibsen's short story, *A Doll's House*, about the housewife, Nora, who breaks with the stereotypical mould of everyday life and leaves her husband and children for a new life. But what kind of life? The ending is never resolved.

So what is to become of storytelling in relation to branding? Here the ending is also open. One thing, however, is for sure: we have reached a point where companies – like Nora – have to break with the prevailing conditions and think in radically new ways. The time of the rational argument is gone. Emotions are taking over. Development and progress require new ways of thinking. The brand has to drive the company forward, and storytelling is the engine that can get the movement going.

Rational businessmen and women who are most at home with boxes and diagrams, are afraid of this development. Meanwhile, our visionary leaders purposefully stride towards a future full of hope. The fact is, there have never been as many exciting possibilities in terms of communication as there are today.

Those companies, who understand how to benefit from story-telling in communicating the values of their brand, are in a strong position.

In a surplus society, companies have to tell a strong story that clearly explains how they make a difference. It must be a story that we can remember and pass on, and one in which we can get involved. For this to happen, management must be prepared to tear down the walls that divide departments in categories and free the entire company to support the same unified story.

In a surplus society, companies have to tell a strong story that clearly explains how they make a difference.

Hopefully, this book has opened a door. Maybe it has planted a seed that will enable your company to start telling its own story. The opportunities abound and the landscape lies wide open. The ending is all up to you.

Bibliography

BOOKS

Branson, Richard (1998): *Losing My Viginity.* Virgin Books.
Carlzon, Jan (1987): *Moments of Truth.* Harpercollins.
Denning, Stephen (2001): *The Springboard.* KMCI Press.
Godin, Seth (1999): *Permission Marketing.* Simon & Schuster.
Jensen, Rolf (1999): *The Dream Society.*
Jyllands-Postens Erhvervsbøger.
McKee, Robert (1997): *Story.* ReganBooks.
Neuhauser, Peg C. (1993): *Corporate Legends & Lore: the power of storytelling as a management tool.*
Pearson, Carol S. & Mark, Margaret (2001):
The Hero and the Outlaw. McGraw-Hill Education.
Peters, Tom & Austin, Nancy (1985): *A Passion for Excellence.* Random House.
Ridderstråle, Jonas & Nordström, Kjell (2000):
Funky Business. ft.com.
Saunders, Dave (1999): *C 20th Advertising.*
Carlton Books Limited.
Simmons, Annette (2001): *The Story Factor.*
Perseus Publishing.

ARTICLES

Bedbury, Scott (2002): "Nine Ways to Fix a Broken Brand". *Fast Company,* issue 55.
Cox, Beth (1998): "Calvin Klein Campaign Features E-Mail Element". *Internetnews.com.*
DeSalvo, Kathy (2001): "BMW Weaves Through The Web With Five Filmmakers". Shoot, Published weekly by BPI Communications.
Errico, Marcus (1998): "Pamela Anderson Gets Bottled" *Eonline.*
Goddard, Ken (1998): "Silver Bottle Helps Strike Gold". *VR Beverage Packaging.*

Hiles, Andrew (2002): "Enterprise Risk & Security Management". *Kingswell International.*

Holmes, Stanley (2001): "Starbucks: Keeping the Brew Hot". *Online Extra.*

Jensen, Rolf (2001): "The Dream Society II". *Instituttet for Fremtidsforskning.*

Lambert, Joe: "What is digital storytelling?". *Center For Digital Storytelling.*

Manjoo, Farhad (2002): "Dying scent of e-mail ad campaign". *Wired News.*

Martin, Michelle (1998): "A dream to the last drop". *The Guardian.*

McCarthy, Michael (2002): "BMW cars to star in online movie sequel". *USA TODAY.*

Mikkelson, Barbara (1999): "Knew Coke". *Snopes.com.*

Ransdell, Eric (2000): "The Nike Story? Just tell it". *Fast Company,* issue 31.

Rubin, Harriet (1998): "How the Best Storytellers Win". *Fast Company,* issue 15.

Shannon, Caitlin (1998): "R.L. Puffer, via e-mail, asks, 'Whatever happened to...? New Coke". *The Christian Science Monitor.*

Snowden, David J. (2000): "The Art and Science of Story". *Business Information Review,* issue 17.

Snowden, David J. (2000): "Story telling: An old skill in a new context". *Business Information Review.*

Span, Paul (1991): "Ads with instant intrigue. For tasters choice, the 45-second soap opera". *Washington Post.*

Stepanek, Marcia (2000): "Tell Me a (digital) story". *Business Week Online.*

Stewart, Thomas A. (1998): "The Cunning Plots of Leadership". *Fortune Magazine.*

Stone, Richard (1999): "How is a business like a story?". *StoryWork Institute.*

Weil, Elizabeth (1998): "Every Leader Tells a Story". *Fast Company,* issue 15.

Wentz, Laurel (1993): "New coffee romance; same old problem". *Advertising Age.*

Yan, Jack (1999): "Nicole and Papa: A 1990s retrospective". *CapOnline, Jyanet.com.*

OTHER

Chandy, Caroline & Thursby-Pelham, Douglas (1992): "Renault Clio: Adding Value During a Recession". Agency Publicis. Advertising Effectiveness Awards.

LEGO Company (2000): "Play for Life". Corporate Image Brochure.

McCann Erickson (1996): "Love over gold - the untold story of TV's greatest romance". Advertising Effectivness Awards. Institute of Practitioners of Advertising.

Starbucks presse release (2003): "Starbucks Seeking Matches Made Over Coffee".

Index

About the Authors

The authors are specialists in strategic communication, branding and storytelling at the European based communication unit SIGMA. Since it was founded in 1996, SIGMA has been dedicated to pursuing good stories for a wide variety of companies on internal and external projects, nationally as well as internationally. Several of the cases in this book are the results of SIGMA's own work. More information about SIGMA can be found at www.sigma.dk.

Klaus Fog

Klaus Fog has worked within storytelling throughout his career, starting out as Marketing Director at leading Danish newspapers, Politiken and Ekstra Bladet. He co-founded the Danish division of Saatchi & Saatchi before being appointed Scandinavian Vice President at TV3 (a Nordic television group) in 1988. Following his work here, he went on to contribute to the turn-around of the Danish national TV station, TV2, as Sales & Marketing Director. In 1996 Klaus Fog founded SIGMA, specialising in strategic communication, branding and storytelling. SIGMA has worked with a diverse number of international clients including: the LEGO Company, Oracle, Oticon, ECCO, and Grundfos. Klaus Fog is an esteemed lecturer and co-author of the book *Franchising - a business model for the future* (1985). Klaus Fog has a Masters Degree in Business Administration.

Christian Budtz

Christian Budtz has a Masters Degree in Communication. He was formerly head of the Student Organisation under the Danish Marketing Association, and freelance journalist at the leading Danish youth magazine, Chili. At SIGMA, Christian

Budtz has specialised in storytelling and strategic communication for a number of accounts, including ECCO and Oracle - and was the driving force behind a global project for the LEGO Company, in which storytelling was used for communicating the brand values internally. Christian Budtz has written several articles about storytelling for key Danish business publications such as Borsen.

Baris Yakaboylu

Baris Yakaboylu has a Master of Science (Design & Communication Management) and solid international experience in the field of storytelling. From his former base in New York, he contributed to the promotion of the Danish corporate sector with Invest in Denmark. He was later put in charge of branding Denmark within the American market as New Media Manager at the Danish Tourist Board, using digital storytelling as a key component. After his return to Denmark, Baris Yakaboylu has specialised in strategic communication and storytelling for a number of accounts such as ECCO, Coloplast and the LEGO Company.